AF407701

Seasonal Workamping for a Living

How We Did It

By: Levi Henley and Natalie Flores-Henley

For our moms, Beverly and Mary Lou

ACKNOWLEDGEMENTS

There were many people, some fellow RVers and some family members, that helped make this book a possibility. We'd like to take this opportunity to thank Beverly Henley, E. Catherine Flores, Julie Chickery, Debby Bradford, Edith Cagle, Jim "Fitz" Fitzpatrick, and Reenie Montgomery. Thank you for the time you put into reading each section and accompanying revisions. Your encouraging words, meticulous edits, and invaluable critiques helped us to reorganize, reevaluate, and recommit content material. Your time and thoughts are greatly appreciated. Thank you!

CONTENTS

INTRODUCTION

Thank you for reading our book. We are Levi and Natalie Henley, full-time RVers and seasonal workampers. If you are new to workamping, you may be wondering why we spelled that word incorrectly. You won't find the word in Webster's dictionary, but you will see it listed in Wikipedia. Spend enough time around full-time RVers, and you are bound to see and hear it eventually. Until a company called Workamper News coined the term in 1987, there was never an official title given to this unique way of life. "Workamper" is a registered trademark now widely used by RVers.

Workamper News is an organization that helps RVers find short and long term, remote and destination-specific jobs all over the nation. The term workamper has become an official title for the livelihood of hundreds of thousands of seasonal and full-time RVers who live and travel all over. Many other groups and websites advertise workamping jobs, including CoolWorks, Workers on Wheels, and the Volunteer.gov portal.

Workamping is a way of life for RVers who have taken to the road or settled in one location. Singles, couples, families, and roommates can be classified as workampers by having a job, or volunteer assignment while residing in a motorhome, travel trailer, fifth wheel, conversion bus or van, you name it. (If you want to get technical, workampers also include folks that work and camp out of a tent or onsite lodging.) Like the all-American dream, your livelihood is your oyster. You fund your travels however you desire.

Some people choose to have jobs they can work remotely from the comfort of their RV, customizing a work schedule of their own and free to pick up and travel as they please (e.g., software developer, social media specialist). Others have jobs that send them to various places based on company needs (e.g., traveling nurse, traveling industrial pipe welder).

A popular category of workamping is seasonal employment. Seasonal workamping positions can be at various locations including campgrounds, farms/ranches, state and national parks, warehouses, lighthouses, marinas, and hotels/resorts. Duties can vary as well. Some are clerical work, outside maintenance, ranch hand, cook, activities organizer, packer/shipper, guide, retail/salesperson, wait staff, or shift manager. The possibilities are endless, but many jobs require skills involving some degree of customer service and collaboration with co-workers.

Job listings range from volunteer positions that include free sites and hook-ups to salaried positions that include health insurance and additional compensations. The length of employment varies and can be as short as a two-week stint or as long as year-round. Most companies hire during their peak seasons: campgrounds and resorts need help during the summer months while Amazon Fulfillment Centers hire more hands during the holidays to meet increased customer orders.

By the time this book is published, we will have funded our travels through seasonal workamping for well over five, going on six years. In that time, what feels like a blink of an eye, we will have workamped in 11 states and worked almost 20 jobs. In the process, we visited national parks and forests, historical markers, popular attractions, yummy eateries, small towns, and beach fronts in nearly twenty-five states, many in the Midwest.

For us, a typical year includes working at a busy campground or tourist destination during the spring/summer months. Most of these positions include 30-40 hours of work per week per person, and we can see crowds of over a thousand people on weekends and holidays. We prefer jobs "up north" so we can beat the grueling heat of the South.

Winters aren't necessarily in warmer climates. While many RVers flock to the tip of Florida and Texas beginning around October/November, you'll find us in states as far north as Tennessee or Kansas. Although we have worked at campgrounds during the holiday season, we've mainly chosen jobs that involve preparation for the hustle and bustle of the holiday season. These jobs involved handling inventory and orders at Amazon, selling pumpkins and Christmas trees at a neighborhood lot, or decorating residential homes and businesses with holiday lights and other novelties.

Each of our workamping jobs has been unique in regards to job responsibilities, management, benefits, location, and culture. We see every job not as a separate event but more as a continuous experience. What we learn from a job, we can apply to the next. Our network of fellow RVers grows, as does learning about the ever-evolving world of the nomad. There are many more companies and positions that we want to try. We have merely glimpsed some of the possibilities for seasonal workamping.

As we discussed writing this book, we thought, *what would have helped us before taking to the road and beginning our seasonal jobs?* We have answered that question by telling our story of seasonal workamping.

This book has four sections. The first section is our story, how we became full-time RVers and eventual seasonal workampers. The second section details jobs we have worked each season. The third part focuses on finding, applying for, and landing your first and next workamping jobs. Finally, section four answers questions and concerns regarding arriving at the job site, how workamping affects taxes, budgeting aspects, and lessons we have learned as seasonal workampers.

You will notice that a lot of the narration looks to be from my (Levi's) point of view. Although written in that format, we both collaborated, wrote, rewrote, argued over, agreed upon, disagreed upon, stopped speaking to each other, apologized, and continued to work on every sentence and paragraph you will read.

A few obligatory notes, we mention several businesses throughout these pages. We have worked for many of these companies, and there are organizations that we find quite useful as full-time RVers. Natalie and I are in no way affiliated with or representing any of these companies. We are simply detailing our experiences with these separate entities.

If you have not had enough of us by the time you finish the book, we chronicle our full-time RVing life, workamping gigs, RV tips, and places we've visited on our website HenleysHappyTrails.com. There you can join our mailing list to get our monthly newsletter. You can check us out on YouTube as well. For now, though, cozy up with a warm blanket and drink; it's storytime.

SECTION ONE:

The CliffsNotes of Our Story

AN IDEA TURNED INTO A REALITY

My wife Natalie and I have been full-time RVers since 2014. Before we took on the nomadic lifestyle, we lived in Las Vegas, owned our first house, and had a few cats and a dog. Vegas was our home for eleven years, but we wanted a change. We knew we wanted to move away from the *entertainment Capital of the World* at some point, but we didn't know where we wanted to go.

We would investigate one place or another, researching online or talking to friends and coworkers, looking to see if there was any place that piqued our interest. We'd take weekend trips to corners of Nevada, road trips to nearby California, and flights to popular destinations like Honolulu and New York City. They were all fun escapes, but they were too short and only gave us enough time to see the main tourist attractions. On top of that, they were pretty expensive.

To curb the ho-hum of our everyday routines, we purchased a small 14-foot travel trailer. It was a huge step up from the Ozark tent we'd purchased from Walmart, and it was what we spent our days off in camping at Lake Mead and Mount Charleston.

Feeling a bit more confident with traveling and camping in the trailer, we planned a trip out of state. We set the GPS northbound to Longview, Washington, to visit family. We traveled up the California, Oregon, and Washington coasts to get there.

Along the way, we were treated to some of the most beautiful places we had ever seen, from the charming coastal towns to the majestic mountains. We savored freshly baked bread and sweet-smelling taffy at roadside stores. We stopped to pick wild blackberries by the ocean. We ate lunch overlooking a beach scene that you only find in paintings; ironically, a woman was painting the scene on canvas not too far from us.

The experience was life-changing. On the way home, Natalie said, "What else haven't we seen?" It was then that we both realized why it was so hard to find a place to move to next. We didn't know what was out there. The conversations turned to "what if" back and forth banter. What if we took a year off to explore the country in an RV? What if we found a way to travel for a living?

At that point, we hadn't planned on doing any of that. There was no feasible way we could take a year off. Natalie worked as a public school teacher, and I was juggling two jobs, one at a scuba shop and another at a tour company. We didn't have the time or the funds to take an extended hiatus. It was just one of those hopeful dreaming conversations, similar to talking about what you would do with the money if you won the lottery.

It didn't stay a dream for long, though. After a few weeks, settled in our home, and regularly scheduled programs in Las Vegas, Natalie brought the subject up again. She had been trying to find ideas from the internet on how we might take an "extended" RV trip. She had stumbled upon a couple who ran a website, rv-dreams.com. She talked about how they, as well as others, travel the country full-time. She had become hooked, and I had to admit it was growing on me, too.

WORKAMPING MEANS EXACTLY WHAT IT SAYS

Fast forward several months and we were both reading books and bookmarking any blog or website about full-time RVing. In the process, we stumbled across this thing called *workamping* (also referred to as work camping). Odd term, we thought, but it means exactly what it says, work while you camp. We wondered if that could be the ticket to our RV dream, the way to afford to travel around North America before we retired.

Although there are easily a dozen organizations that devote the bulk of their services to helping full-time and seasonal RVers find jobs in and around the nation, the first company we were introduced to by veteran RVers was Workamper News. We quickly joined the free tier of their membership options, which allowed access to daily employment ads online and their bi-monthly publication, also available online.

We looked through past Workamper News magazines and listings of jobs and realized there were a lot of workamping jobs out there, all over the country. We just had to figure out how to get hired. At that point, the idea of picking up and leaving Las Vegas to travel the country had moved from being a dream to a possible reality.

We decided we needed a plan. We talked about timelines and how much money we would need to save up to start. We tried to plan when we were going to buy an RV and simultaneously sell our home. We knew our travel trailer was a bit small to live in. After scouring RV forums, checking out RV lots, and attending multiple RV shows, we determined that a small Class A Motorhome was the right setup for our little family.

It took us three years to put aside our feelings of apprehension and doubt and put our plans in action. We bit the bullet, sold almost all of our possessions and used some of the profits we made from selling our home and belongings to make a down payment on a gently used motorhome.

HOW WE GOT OUR FIRST WORKAMPING JOBS

One of our biggest insecurities about starting the full-time RV lifestyle was figuring out how to land our first job. We kept thinking the odds were not in our favor considering hundreds of people must be applying to the same companies. Questions like that were ever-present while we planned to become nomads. They were the questions that reminded us we were taking chances.

We learned about some of the more popular workamping gigs that happen each year. The one that caught our eye was Amazon CamperForce. Amazon hires hundreds of RVers every year for several of its shipping facilities during the holiday season. We thought this had to be an easier job to land than a campground that only hires a handful of workers.

Amazon wouldn't be our first workamping job. We were out of our home and living in our RV by the end of 2014. Natalie would be resigning from the school district in June of 2015. We needed a summer job before starting Amazon in the fall.

We started doubling our efforts, looking through Workamper News job ads in search of a summer job. It was a daunting task, mostly because we didn't feel like we had very much work experience with most of the jobs advertised.

We'd comb through many ads that looked like this:

> *RV Park*
> *We are looking for a couple with good communication skills to fill maintenance and office positions. Knowledge of Campground Master is a plus.*

Some of the ads had more detail, but many read generally the same. Thoughts raced through my mind after reading a few. I'm pretty good with computers, but I've never considered myself a "maintenance" type of person. Even though I can mow lawns and troubleshoot minor problems like replacing faucets in a house or recognizing a tripped breaker, I didn't feel qualified. The "Campground Master" experience was a red flag as well. A lot of ads wanted people experienced in particular campground registration programs, and we, of course, had never heard of the software.

For many reasons, we wanted our first workamping job to be in Nevada. As luck would have it, we spotted a job ad for camp hosts at an established RV park in Fernley, Nevada, Desert Rose RV Park. We were so determined to land this job because of its location that we refrained from looking at any other ads.

That would be the one! The ad, like so many others, wished for both an experienced maintenance person and an office attendant with strong computer skills. We didn't have the previous experience, but we dressed up our resumes to accentuate the skills that we figured would translate to the ones requested. We swallowed our doubts about the possibility of getting hired and emailed everything requested in the ad, our resume with a photo of us and our rig.

A few days later, we received an email from the owner of Desert Rose RV park telling us that she wanted to set up a phone interview. We were honest with the owner and explained that we were new to full-time RVing and the workamping scene. We also were not shy to mention that we did not have experience with working in a campground, but we were willing to learn. By the end of the phone call, we had pretty much secured the job as camp hosts. We were going to Fernley for the summer!

Our next step was completing online applications to work with Amazon CamperForce. This procedure was completely different from our application process with the campground, as it was all completed online.

We waited a bit longer to learn about our confirmed employment, but we eventually heard back and were over the moon to know that we had secured not one but two workamping gigs before officially taking off on the road as full-time RVers!

Our anxiety and fears towards job hunting were melting away. Finding jobs and getting hired was most definitely possible. We were overthinking the application process and underestimating our capabilities. It was time to throw away those doubts and embrace the workamping life!

SECTION TWO:

Workamping through the Seasons

SPRING/SUMMER WORK

At this point, you know the story that followed our first two workamping jobs. We continued to find jobs and fund our travels. It is common for us to work three to four different jobs a year, basically one job per season. To give you an idea of the options when planning a year of workamping, we decided to give a run-down of the different types of jobs we have worked throughout the seasons.

We will give some background about the jobs, what the duties and responsibilities entailed, compensation, and our take on the experience. We'll also include an anecdote on a typical work-day. We hope you will have a grasp of the jobs that are out there by the time you finish Section Two. Later, in Section Three, we will go into detail about how we found and applied to these seasonal workamping jobs.

Spring/Summer Work

Campgrounds

Working at an RV park is one of the first jobs that come to mind for many when mentioning seasonal workamping. We have worked at five different campgrounds over the years. That is about one campground job per year. They are familiar territory to us, and depending on the position, can allow a break with the hectic hours we put in during the holiday season. Truthfully, camp-ground jobs are not strictly spring/summer jobs, but the time of year that offers the most openings is during the summer months between Memorial Day and Labor Day.

A campground experience can vary widely since RV parks come in all different shapes and sizes. Some only hire two couples and have less than a hundred sites. Other parks hire over twenty people and have more than a thousand sites. Larger parks have all sorts of amenities like shops, cafes, and a water park. Some workampers prefer the intimacy of the smaller campgrounds while others thrive on the busy atmosphere of the larger resorts. We prefer the latter.

Duties

The most common job title for campground jobs is the camp host. Larger campgrounds will list other positions such as housekeeping, store clerk, front desk staff, gate guard, and many others. We have worked many of the different job duties campgrounds have to offer.

For the most part, though, it's safe to put camp hosts into two categories: outside maintenance and office staff. Maintenance duties may include: cleaning the campsite, mowing and edging of sites, picking up trash, disinfecting bathrooms and laundry facilities, filling propane tanks, escorting guests to sites, repairing outside equipment, painting, etc. Some work ads may request applicants with specialty skills like electrical training or carpentry.

Working in the office can include taking reservations over the phone or online, registering incoming campers, maintaining office cleanliness, sorting mail, operating general office machines, and assisting with customer requests, concerns, and complaints. Often the park has a small store in the "office" area and will sell basic camping and food items to make the camping experience more comfortable.

Those may seem like overwhelming lists, and some of the task descriptions may make you feel like you don't have any experience in that area. We have found that most campgrounds are willing to train employees on tasks as necessary.

On some occasions, both Natalie and I have been hired for

positions with zero background history or training. For example, I once helped pave roads in a campground using giant chip and tar machines. Natalie operated a tractor and was sent out into a campground, hauling a pump machine to pump out RV waste tanks.

In both of those instances, training was offered with machinery and actual tasks. It was also understood that we would not be fast or perfect right off the bat. We have never been afraid to tell the park owners when we felt out of our comfort zone, and they have always been understanding and helpful in those times.

Hours and Compensation

The hours of a campground job vary. Some are only looking for 15 to 20 hours a week per employee, while others request 35 to 40 hours a week per person. If you are traveling with a partner, you will most likely have the same days off. One of our favorite schedules we had at a park was three nine-hour days on and three days off. For the most part, it is quite easy to find a campground job that offers the hours you would like.

The compensation varies quite a bit in campground jobs. Some jobs are on a volunteer basis, and others offer payment. Usually, volunteer positions are no more than 20 hours a week per person. A full hookup site and utilities can be the exchange or payment for these hours worked.

The average paid campground position seems to pay between $9 and $11 per hour. Your RV site is usually free or deeply discounted. The max we paid for a site while working at a park was $150 a month. Water and sewer have always been included for us, but electric charges were sometimes a separate fee. Out of five RV parks, we have paid for electric usage in two of them. One offered a stipend of $100 a month towards electricity and charged for anything we used above that. The other charged full price.

Many campgrounds offer additional perks besides hourly compensation and an RV site. These may include free or discounted laundry, access to park amenities like the pool, golf course (mini and full size) or boat rentals, discounted store products, free or discounted tickets to local attractions, and propane at wholesale price. When you add everything the campground is offering, it will effectively increase your dollars per hour earned.

A cautionary note, this positive can swing to a negative depending upon the park. We have seen many advertisements that offer the higher end of pay, say $11 an hour or more, but you have to pay for the site and electricity. Others will have you exchange a certain number of your hours per week for the site before they start paying you hourly. Not all those types of jobs are bad deals, but some can drop your effective hourly wage to well below minimum wage once you do the math. It just depends on what you want in a job. Workampers vary in needs, income, savings, etc. What makes one person/couple happy may not work for another.

Our first workamping job at Desert Rose RV Park, for example, traded a certain number of hours for the site before the pay kicked in. However, we were given free laundry and free electricity in the hot Nevada summer. The money we saved versus the cost of the site was a net positive for us once we did the math. The important take here is to make sure you always do the math and decide if a position is a good fit for your needs and budget.

Our Experience

We have found that campgrounds are a great source of workamping income. It may take some time to learn the layout of a new park, especially if it is a large one. Each location will have different rules, but for the most part, they start to overlap. The nice thing about workamping at campgrounds is that they all operate relatively the same so you can move from one job to another without a huge learning curve.

It's nice not having to commute to work as well. Step out of your RV, and you are at work. This convenience can be kind of a double-edged sword too. A campground that you live and work at every week can get old very fast.

We experience this more so in small RV parks. However friendly and welcoming the atmosphere, living and working in an RV park can feel like swimming in a fishbowl. There is little privacy. Separating work lives from personal lives can be a challenge with co-workers and RV park guests. Even though the sign in front of your RV may say "off duty," people will still knock on your door. Some workampers thrive on this social interaction, and some are homebodies and value their quiet downtime.

We have had some great experiences working with other RVers as camp hosts. We have also had issues where we didn't quite jive with some. To separate our work lives from our personal lives, we try to make a point to leave our place of work on at least one of our days off, so we don't feel like we are at work all the time.

A Day in The Life of...

In small campgrounds, I typically worked outside, and Natalie worked in the office. Once we stepped out of our RV in the morning, we were at work. Natalie headed to the office and opened up. Opening the office included counting a cash drawer, checking any notes left by the previous shift, and looking at the day's scheduled arrivals. At most places, she gave the outside help (just me at smaller campgrounds) a paper detailing which sites to checkout for the day.

Throughout the day, she took phone calls, made reservations when people called in, separated the mail into customer's mailboxes, or sometimes delivered mail directly to their rig. She was essentially the store clerk, office manager, customer service representative, and maintenance dispatcher all rolled into one.

While Natalie worked in the office, I retrieved the golf cart, did a quick drive around the park, and checked the bathrooms to see if something needed my immediate attention. I ended my round at the office, where I got the checkout paper for the day.

I drove around the campground, checking off who had already vacated their spot. Some parks had electric meters that needed to be read whenever someone checked out. Other parks would only do this for people staying longer than a week. Whatever the case, they all had some system in place to ensure people checked out at the required time.

RVers were good about leaving at the designated time, but some days I had to remind a couple of stragglers about the checkout time. My next task was usually determined by any notes Natalie collected from management. Sometimes there was a leaky faucet or broken something or other that I needed to check out. If I could fix it, I did. If it was beyond my capability, I did what I could and let the park manager or owners know what the problem was so they could contact the appropriate people.

If there were no pending tasks, I filled my day with picking up waste from pet runs, cleaning bathrooms and showers, wiping down laundry rooms, scooping out ash from fire pits, and other janitorial tasks. Throughout the day, I got several calls from Natalie, over a walkie talkie, to check customer concerns, escort people to their sites, fill propane tanks, and any other customer service-related issues that came up.

At the end of the day, it was time for Natalie to record sales, clean up the office, and post the closed sign before locking up the office. I put away any tools or supplies used for the day and parked the golf cart.

Tourist Hot Spots

Every state, it seems, has an assortment of big attractions like national parks, theme parks, wineries, scenic drives, and caves. Summer is the busy season for many tourist destinations, and quite a few companies hire workampers for these hot spots.

Amusement parks like Adventureland in Iowa and Dollywood in Tennessee have workamper programs. Workampers are hired at retail shops and restaurants surrounding natural wonders like Yellowstone, Grand Teton, and the Grand Canyon. Help is also needed within the parks.

These places offer hours of engaging activities, striking scenery, and rich history; it's no wonder why so many people flock to these locations for days or weeks to quickly cram in as much sightseeing as possible. In contrast, when you workamp at these locations, you get to live there, soak in all the area has to offer, and truly experience why these places attract so many people.

One such place for us is the Black Hills of South Dakota. There is so much to see and do there; it's delightfully dizzying. It also happens to be one of the most beautiful places we have seen in the United States. Over a dozen well-known attractions, like Mt. Rushmore and Custer State Park, all piled in one concentrated area, make the Black Hills a prime tourist spot. Many businesses in the area hire workampers to help meet the demands of the visitor influx. We were hired to help meet the demands at a local winery in the Black Hills called Prairie Berry Winery.

Over the years, this family-owned business has expanded to include a microbrewery, restaurant, events center, and various community activities throughout the year. Between Memorial Day and Labor Day, the winery alone has recorded up to 2000 customers entering the winery daily, especially on holidays and during special events like the Sturgis Motorcycle Rally.

Duties

Our job title was wine tasting associates. We worked behind the bar yapping away with customers and serving samples, ringing up and boxing or bagging one sale after the next, taking down orders and charging guests at the kitchen counter, greeting guests at the door, serving wine and cheese samples at the pairing station, grabbing more cases of wine from the back storage room, and stocking merchandise. A lot was going on most of the time, and we were always moving.

Hours and Compensation

Many of the workamping jobs in these tourist hot spots are similar. Most of them involve retail or customer service. Expect to work anywhere from 30 to 40 hours a week. With our job, pay started at $11 an hour, and there was an opportunity for a raise after training.

Many RV parks in tourist areas are rather expensive. We received a stipend that paid a portion of our RV site each month, and we found that the RV park they recommended was very reasonable for the area.

When we are looking into jobs in tourist areas, we take into consideration how much we have to pay for our site. It doesn't make sense for us to pay $800+ a month plus the cost of relocating hundreds or even thousands of miles to get to a job for $10 or $11 an hour for a few months.

As with any workamping job, there are often accompanying perks in addition to the site and wages. Winery merchandise and food were available at half price. At many locations in the Black Hills, including Prairie Berry, employees receive a green VIP card that grants deeply discounted or free admission to the area's many attractions.

The Black Hills and Badlands Tourism Association recognizes that one of their best advertisers for the area's attractions are the frontline workers who interact with the tourists. Participating businesses disperse VIP cards to their employees so that they can visit many of the area attractions and share those experiences with others. We took advantage of this and saved hundreds of dollars!

Our Experience

During our time as wine tasting associates, we learned a lot about the process of making wine, and of course, tasting it as well. We found an appreciation for nontraditional fruit wines which that particular winery produced. It was kind of fun being able to work in an industry we had previously known very little about.

Working in a place that requires you to interact with and give presentations to five hundred or more people in one eight-hour period is a whole different kind of exhausted. It can leave you feeling mentally numb and without a voice.

Overall this workamping job was worth it to us for the pay we received. We plan on working other jobs like it in the future. We enjoy being able to live in and explore these amazing locations that many people only get to visit for a few days.

A Day in The Life of...

There were overlapping shifts at Prairie Berry. With the opening shift, we arrived in the morning about an hour before the winery opened to the public. There were about three crew members, and we each worked on portions of a checklist. These items included preparing the jelly sample table, stocking the wine coolers, placing napkins, straws, and glasses at the restaurant counter, filling empty shelves with more bottles of wine, and arranging lawn games.

We were assigned our position for the day, which could be at the tasting bar, cash register, lunch counter, or at the front doors greeting patrons. On busier days, someone would be assigned to man a cheese and wine pairing station. For the most part, our day's assignment remained the same, but as co-workers took their lunches, we would be asked to cover someone's position for a while. There were more wine tasting positions than anything else, so you were likely to be behind a bar.

As customers came through the doors, they were directed to a bar for a tasting. Once they stepped up to the bar, we would tell them a little history about the winery using a memorized script. We were encouraged to make the presentation our own, so we each had a custom speech complete with jokes and little side stories.

Once they were acquainted with the history of the winery, customers were handed a checklist of the available wines, and they could select up to five to try. Some customers knew what they wanted from the get-go, while others wanted a description of each wine. Some people were only interested in a certain type of wine, so we would point out that particular category of wine from the list.

Each wine was unique in its ingredients, name origin, and taste. It sounds like a lot to memorize, especially learning all of these attributes for 15-20 separate bottles of wine. However, after the hundredth customer, talking about each wine became second nature. We had not fully digested all of the information before stepping behind the bar for the first time, but we had our notes to refer to.

Wine bottles used for sampling at the bar were set up with pourers that dispensed accurate sample portions. This convenient mechanism took care of the measuring component of our job, giving us more time to juggle the large groups. It wasn't unheard of for one associate to have ten to fifteen customers at once. On holidays or weekends, there would be groups waiting behind groups at the bar for their turn at samples.

The winery had three main bars. Three or four associates shared a bar. It was important to be alert and avoid bumping into one another. As I sailed from one customer to the next, it felt like I was an auctioneer spouting off the same stories in rapid-fire succession. This repetitive action could go on for hours some days. We had bottled water and could take short breaks if needed.

The afternoon shift did not have the advantage of easing into their workday. The pandemonium was already in full swing as they entered the winery. They usually started at the bar, relieving co-workers for their lunch break. Opening shifts ended around 5 or 6 PM and closing shifts popped in around 1 or 2 PM.

About an hour before the closing shift ended, the doors were shut and locked. The night shift began clean-up. The wine bars were wiped down, the lawn games were stored away, bathrooms were disinfected, and the dining chairs were turned upside down and sat atop their respective table before the floor was mopped. The managers counted the cash drawers, and the kitchen staff finished the dishes before everyone went home to relax and do it all over again the next day.

FALL/WINTER WORK

Sugar Beet Harvest

October is the starting point for the sugar beet harvest, encompassing areas of the Upper Midwest like Montana, North Dakota, and Minnesota. For at least a week or two (some seasons extending to the Thanksgiving holiday), trucks filled to the brim with beets traverse the towns delivering their cargo to a designated receiving station, only to repeat the process several more times.

At the receiving (also referred to as piling) stations, the beets are piled twenty-five feet high and are stored in those piles until they are brought to the refinery to make sugar. A piling station can be brimming with activity. Trucks rush in to and away from their drops, the beets roar up a conveyor belt into an ever-growing pile, ground crews rush to check grower tickets and fill beet sample bags, and the machine operators whirl around cleaning up debris.

Who makes this grand event possible? That would be American Crystal Sugar Company and its adjoining corporation, Sidney Sugars. Thousands of farmers in the surrounding areas buy into the conglomerate, growing, transporting, and profiting from their bounty. Express Employment Professionals serves as the hiring agency, gathering workers, RVers and locals alike, to assist with the collecting and storing end of the production.

The sugar beet harvest is a race against Mother Nature to collect and deliver beets in just the right conditions. If it's too warm, the beets start to rot as their temperature rises. If it's too cold, frost can damage the beets. If it's too wet, trucks can get stuck in the beet fields.

Most positions are at the piling stations. There are three main positions at a piling station: boom operator, piler operator, and helper/sample taker.

- The piler operator runs the piling machine by signaling the truckers when to dump their loads and working various levers in the machine to ensure the beets run through at the right pace.

- The boom is a long arm with a conveyor belt that carries beets from the piler and distributes them on top of the pile evenly. The boom operator works this part of the piling machine.

- The helper/sample taker marks each truck ticket with their piler's designated number. If the truck driver hands over a sample ticket, the helper collects a sample from the truckload. This sample is obtained from the piling machine. As the beets run through the piler, the helper presses a button that directs a small load of beets down a chute and into a sample bag. The bag is tagged with the sample ticket and set aside to be gathered up and sent to a lab for quality check.

Outside of the piling station, there are also a limited number of jobs available in the labs where the quality of beets from different farmers is sampled. We completed two consecutive seasons. In the first season, we were both helpers/sample takers. The second year, I was a skid steer operator, and Natalie worked in the scale house.

To those RVers returning year after year, the benefits outweigh the adverse conditions. The actual tasks are not difficult to complete; it's the matter of endurance that proves challenging. As a worker, you may experience the following.

Fatigue and Cold Weather: The shifts are 12 hours a day, 7 days a week until harvest is over. Standing on a concrete slab in the cold for 12 hours a day can cause quite a bit of fatigue. If you're lucky, you will get a few days off due to the weather being too hot, wet, or cold. When I say cold, that would be in the low 20s, which is around -5 Celsius for any Canadians reading this. Too hot is anything above 54°F (12°C). That means that optimal working conditions are from cold to freezing, not counting the windchill factor. We made sure to bring plenty of layers and would frequently take some off or put them on throughout our shifts to stay comfortable.

Since we worked long days, we didn't always feel like preparing dinner when we got home. We found that making casseroles and soups allowed us to have hot leftovers for several days and brought warmth and comfort on our lunch breaks.

Dirty Clothes: The soil around the worksite is very claylike. It sticks to everything. It layers on your boots, and you have to scrape it off every twenty minutes or so. It sticks to clothes, hard hats, and safety goggles. Don't wear anything you are particularly attached to. If you aren't careful, all that dirt can end up in your car and RV.

We learned that lesson our first year, and the following year we placed a box in the back of our car. We took off any outer layers, including our shoes, and put those in a box after our shift. We changed into clean sneakers before driving home and put the dirty outer layers on once we arrived at the job site the next day.

Loud Noises: The piling machines run 24 hours a day. Tractors, trucks, bobcats, and other machinery zip around everywhere. The piling stations are very noisy. The company provides earplugs, but even then, the constant noise can feel maddening by your tenth 12-hour shift in a row. You almost don't realize how loud the area is until the machines are turned off for a few brief moments for maintenance or a quick repair.

Porta-Potties: There are no bathrooms on site except for porta-potties. With long shifts, it's pretty much a guarantee you will have to use them. If you happen to get the night shift, we recommend keeping a small flashlight or headlamp with you because the porta-potties don't have lights in them. We were apprehensive about them upon first arriving at the job site, but they are frequently cleaned out. With the cold weather, they didn't really tend to smell either.

Possible Pet Issues: Many RVers travel with their pets. Pets are not allowed at the piling station, even in your vehicle. At the time we worked at the sugar beet harvest, we had three cats and a dog. As exhausted as we were, we took our dog out for long walks in the RV park before and after our shifts. There was the option to ask fellow workampers working opposite shifts and even the campground host to let our dog out for bathroom breaks while we were at work.

We ended up keeping a few pee pads in the RV in case she had to go. She was a very nervous girl, and we didn't feel comfortable having someone open the RV door to let her out. Plus, we feared that one of the cats would bolt out the door. This arrangement worked out for us, and we did the same at our Amazon CamperForce job. (Side note, in two separate workamping seasons, my dad worked with us, and my mom was able to take our dog out while we were working.)

It wasn't all hardship and fatigue. In fact, there were many upsides to our job.

New Skill Sets: Neither of us had worked in any field close to the farming industry before the beet harvest. It worried us at first that we were way out of our element and questioned whether or not we could do well in this job. Turns out, after working alongside locals and other RVers, some novice and some veterans of the harvest, we were able to learn quite a bit in a short time.

I was asked to drive the skid steer to help with cleanup. My foreman asked me if I had ever driven one on our first day. I told him I hadn't but was willing to learn. Apparently, that was enough for him. The following day I was sitting in a classroom watching a video on how to work a skid steer. I was able to practice with the machine before using it around other equipment and people. I picked it up pretty quickly, and now I can add a "skid steer operator" to my resume.

Both Natalie and I were allowed to learn how to work the piling machine as backup piler operators. There is a list of positions and skills one can learn at a piling station, and if you are willing to learn, they will teach you.

Compensation: It is possible to make $2000 to $2500 per person. This varies from year to year and company to company. Our first year was about $13.50 an hour base pay. Employees see an increase in their hourly rate if they return the following year. Anything over 8 hours a day was paid time and a half. All hours worked on Saturdays were paid time and a half, and Sundays were paid double time. A bonus is tacked on for those that finish out the season. Overall we made between $5000 and $6000 in about 16 days in our first year and a little over $8000 in 18 days our second year.

Free Site: Workampers are provided a free site at a campground close to their work location. The amenities vary, and the hookups can be partial or full. For the partial hookup sites, a honey wagon (vehicle used to suction waste from septic tanks) comes to pump out the RVs regularly. We had a full hookup site; however, the park shut off the water in mid-October. The park scheduled a water truck to come twice a week to fill our tanks with fresh water for the remainder of the harvest.

A Day in The Life of...

Like most rookies to the beet harvest, we were helper/sample takers our first season. A typical day at the sugar beet harvest required us to wake up about an hour and a half before our shift. If it was a day shift, that was 6:30AM, and if it was the night shift, that would be 6:30PM. We dressed up in layers. Our outermost layers were typically still in the car along with our shoes, where we left them the prior day.

After eating a quick breakfast, one of us packed our lunch for the day, and the other would take our dog, Brewy, out for a quick walk around the park. Sandwiches and snacks were packed for lunch, but some days we'd bring a microwavable dish (since we had access to a microwave at work).

It was about a 20-minute drive to our piling station. There were two pilers at our site with a team of at least five people per piler. We parked by the scale house where the trucks entered and exited the site. Natalie and I put on our outer layers (coats and overalls), safety vests, hard hats, and work shoes. We clocked in at the scale house and relieved the previous crew by taking over their stations.

Trucks entered the station at the scale house, and their load was weighed. They then pulled up next to the piler and dumped their beets. After unloading, we directed the driver to another section of the machine that returned the dirt from their load. Next, trucks went to the scale house to be weighed with their dirt load. This ensured the growers got paid for their beet deposit.

To maintain a safe work environment, to avoid workers from sliding or trucks from skidding or getting stuck, helpers periodically scraped the claylike mud off the worksite's cement pads using various types of shovels. A skid steer operator performed the larger mess, scooping up beets and large mounds of dirt that fell from the plier.

Lunch and rest breaks were usually decided upon by each crew. On colder days, breaks were more frequent, giving people plenty of chances to warm up in the scale house or their cars. After 12 hours, the replacement crew showed up. If the weather was good, that process was repeated for 14 to 18

Amazon CamperForce

Starting as early as September, Amazon takes in hundreds of workampers and locals in an attempt to meet the demands of customers around the world seeking gifts for the holiday season. They refer to this as peak season. There are many Amazon warehouses all over the nation, and the world for that matter, but only a handful offer peak season positions to RVers. This program is known as Amazon CamperForce.

Those pursuing a seasonal position with Amazon's CamperForce program can expect to do one or more of the following general tasks: receiving, counting, stowing, picking, and/or packing. Natalie and I worked two peak seasons with Amazon CamperForce. We were assigned to the ICQA (Inventory Control Quality Assurance) department for the first season and the stowing department the second season.

Be aware that the department and shift you apply for may not be your assignment. Positions assigned to workampers, ultimately, depend on the need. When Natalie and I originally applied for Amazon CamperForce, I had requested to work in the receiving department during the night shift, and she applied for the picking department during the day shift. We both ended up together, in a completely different department, ICQA, working nights.

For anyone planning on working with Amazon CamperForce, we can offer the following tidbits based on our experience there.

Embrace the mundane work. Every job that you will be given in a warehouse setting has you repeating the same few steps over and over again. The first day or two will feel new with every position, but it will get old fast. It's not a gripe, just the nature of warehouse work. We just had to tell ourselves it was only for a few months.

Expect overtime. After Thanksgiving, the hours can get crazy. It wasn't unusual to work five 10-11 hour shifts a week. If the thought of repeating the same task everyday sounds maddening, try doing it 50-55 hours a week. Again, it was short-lived, and there was a light at the end of the tunnel. We worked the graveyard shift the first time on top of it all, so we were always tired.

Get good shoes. It is a good idea to find the most comfortable shoes you have ever worn. You will be either standing or walking on concrete 40-plus hours a week.

Lap up the monetary benefits. CamperForce is considered among the highest paying workamping jobs. As of 2019, workampers can expect an hourly wage starting at $15. With overtime, this can add up quickly.

Amazon provides a list of campgrounds. They offer a $550 monthly stipend towards campground fees paid directly to the campground. In some cases, the campground charges more than the Amazon stipend, and you will be responsible for paying this difference. Be aware that Amazon's policies change from year to year.

Start networking. Working around hundreds of fellow workampers is great for making friends, getting RV tips, and even hearing about other workamping opportunities. During breaks and lunch periods, we would sit down with other workampers and talk about all things RVing, including past jobs. We learned about other seasonal jobs. We were also encouraged to take a stab at remote working by a fellow RVer who moonlighted as a freelance writer.

A Day in The Life of...

We've worked at a total of two Amazon facilities and had a

different experience each year. The first year we were in a robotic facility, and in the second year, we were in a legacy facility.

The difference between the two was the amount of walking. In the robotic facility, we stood at a station while what looked like an oversized orange Roomba, known as a Kiva, brought over a shelving unit loaded with an assortment of products. The product was brought to us. In contrast, a legacy facility has traditional stationary shelves with products strategically arranged. We walked to the product. Since most of the CamperForce programs have been held in legacy facilities, we'll focus on our second-year experience when we worked as stowers.

We reported to work, five days a week at 6 AM. We "punched in" at a time clock by scanning the barcode on our picture ID badge. We had our badge on throughout the workday, hung around our neck by a lanyard since we needed it to access various devices and software programs to complete different tasks.

After working in the warehouse for a week, we had acclimated somewhat to the loud roaring of the conveyor belts. Earplugs were available to all employees, as well as work gloves, safety blades to open boxes, reflective vests, and painkillers like Tylenol or Ibuprofen. Employees could access these items at vending machines using their badge and free of charge.

Once clocked in, we made our way to our designated meeting spot in the warehouse for our stowing department. Our crew of at least fifty was a combination of CamperForce participants and full-time or seasonal local workers. We'd gather at the beginning of each shift to hear announcements given by one of the managers. Announcements included the production numbers from the day before (e.g., how many orders shipped out, how many products stowed), safety reminders, and goals to shoot towards for the day (e.g., reduce mistakes, refrain from time off-task).

We'd limber up with a few upper and lower body stretches, before picking up a scanner and heading off to our assigned sections of the warehouse. For the most part, Natalie and I worked in the same area, but there were a couple of times where we worked on opposite ends of the facility.

Carts full of merchandise would be prepared by another department in advance and lined up so that it could then be stowed on shelves throughout the warehouse. We'd each grab a cart from our designated area and roll it to an aisle of our choice to commence stowing. We stowed all kinds of items, including pet food, books (it was very tempting to want to read many of them), toys, kitchen appliances, and clothes, so many clothes (most notably underwear and ugly Christmas sweaters).

The stowing procedure was always the same. We used our safety blade to open a box containing products. Using our scanner, we scanned a product from the box and checked to see that the scanner's description of the product matched the actual product. The item was then stowed on an appropriate shelf.

We did this for a few hours before taking a 15-minute break at the closest break room. We'd meet up with other associates and talk about how the day was going or just random chit chat while shoving snacks in our mouth.

Then it was back to our carts and boxes for a few more hours. Once completely finished with a cart, we'd each collect another to work on. If there were any discrepancies in the description or condition of an item, assistance was sought with a problem solver. That person had access to the center's entire inventory and could finagle any issues behind a laptop.

We clocked out for lunch. Lunch was mid-shift and 30 minutes long. We would eat our packed sandwiches or heat up leftovers, chit chat, watch TV, and maybe check our phones (which had to be stored in lockers or our car, outside of the workplace).

After lunch, we clocked in at the time clocks and met up for a mid-day meeting (same place as the morning meeting) for additional announcements.

We returned to the designated station and continued stowing for a few more hours. Most days, empty drawers and compartments were hard to come by, especially for bulky items like coats, hats, or appliances. Finding an open spot took several minutes in those cases. It was always a treat to find empty bins just screaming for products to store.

Our second 15-minute break signaled that our day was almost done. After the break, we returned to your designated work-sites and continued stowing items until the workday came to an end.

Holiday Lot Managers

Another job that many people stumble upon while researching workamping is managing a holiday lot. Firework stands, pumpkin patches, and Christmas tree lots come to mind. We put our customer service, retail, and managerial skills to the test one season when we signed up to run a pumpkin and Christmas tree lot in Memphis, Tennessee. For the sake of simplicity, we'll focus on our experience with the Christmas tree lot.

Companies across the nation, most notably California and Florida, hire RV couples to live at and run Christmas tree lots from November through late December. The companies that own the lots range in size from large corporations to "mom-and-pop" setups.

As holiday lot managers, our job entailed selling Christmas trees, garland, stands, and any number of other Christmas decorations. We oversaw hired help and managed the day to day tasks like recording inventory and sales. Some companies hire and schedule a small staff to help carry and tie trees to customers' cars, while others leave the hiring and scheduling to each lot manager.

In addition to selling holiday products, many lots have some sort of kiddie amusement park complete with rides, a bounce house, games, and other activities that families can enjoy while looking for their perfect Christmas tree. Ensuring that safety rules are followed falls under the duty of the lot manager. Our lot was strictly tree sales, minus the kiddie park.

The job is definitely not a *kick back and relax* kind of job. Running a lot requires hours of setup. We helped stand over 150 trees in cups before the lot even opened. Setting up trees in stands was constant. After a tree was purchased, a new one filled the empty stand. Plus, even with the extra help provided, we were still lifting trees and sending them off with customers. Having said that, every lot manager experience is different, and it is important to clarify information regarding job specifications, lot set-up, and benefits package before agreeing to work the season.

Depending on the company, the degree of labor and hours will vary. It can be up to 12 hours a day, 7 days a week. Since we were working long days and didn't really have the energy to do much outside business hours, we used slow periods during the day to run errands. Usually around noon on some weekdays, Natalie would visit the nearest laundromat, pick up groceries using the store's curbside service, or grab take out.

Most managers are required to live on the lot for the duration. Some locations will provide a full hookup site in a fenced area, and others will provide water and electric sources with a weekly honey wagon service. Our lot was in an open field and our motorhome sat far away from the road, behind the tent. Although we were not surrounded by a fence, we never felt in danger or unsafe. We always locked our door and our belongings and one of us was always on the lot.

Lot managers see extremes in pay from lot to lot and company to company. Payment can include base pay and commission or strictly commission-based. Base pay would include time put towards setting up the lot and hiring staff. Commission percentages vary. Customer traffic and sales can range considerably, depending on the lot location. For example, the "mom-and-pop" company we worked for owned three lots in Memphis. Our lot was in a suburb. We sold more trees that were over eight feet. Another lot located in a busy strip mall sold more accessories like wreaths and garland.

We were on a commission-only contract and made around $6000 at our lot. Our fellow friends and workamping couples have worked with companies that offer base pay and commission and have easily pulled in $10,000 in two months. Lots with an accompanying amusement park have pulled in even more profit.

A Day in The Life of...

About 180 trees were displayed in and around the tent, with many hundreds more laid down behind the tent to replace the standing ones as they were sold. We had all types of trees, including Frasier furs, Noble furs, Douglas pines, Black Hills pines, and Scotch pines. They ranged in height from three-foot tabletop trees to 14-foot behemoths.

Our lot was open from 9 am to 9 pm. We would get up at about 8:00, eat and dress for whatever weather the day had in store. There were quite a few chilly and rainy days. By about 8:45, we would step out of our RV and onto the lot. The closest tree for sale was maybe 15 feet away, so we were really on the lot.

Once out, we would open the gate we had fashioned across the dirt driveway leading into our parking lot. We hung the open sign on a nail we hammered into a post from our makeshift checkout station.

If the previous night was busy, we would fill any cups that were empty with trees from the back. Natalie would normally set up our tablets displaying our Point of Sale (POS) system and layout the sales report charts we also had to fill out. Although one of us was always manning the checkout station, Natalie always wore a fanny pack containing the cash and change.

While we waited for customers, we would take a measuring stick around and price trees we just set out. The owner of the company was very particular about how the trees were priced, and we were given specific instructions on this process. Generally, pricing took into account the type, height, and overall condition of the tree. While it was slow, we allowed our dog, Brewy, to weave in and out of the forest of trees while we priced them. That may have been one of her favorite parts of the day.

The owner hired extra help for each lot some evenings and on weekends when we usually saw an increase in customer traffic. Once customers arrived, we would help them by listening to their requests, suggesting trees that may match their criteria, and completing a tree transaction.

We had bits of information on each tree: the hardiest trees to hang large ornaments, most fragrant, best bargain, etc. Some customers wanted time to browse, and others wanted help examining every tree. Sooner or later, most of them made a decision. If it was a day that I had help, the employees would pick up the tree and give the customer the price tag to give to

Natalie.

The highest percentage of income we got was from accessories like stands, wreaths, and tree additives. Natalie always made sure to point the customers in that direction during the final sale.

While Natalie rang up the customer, one of the lot workers or I would prepare a tree at the cutting station. To ready the tree for its new home, we would use a chainsaw to make a fresh cut on the bottom of the tree, and if the customer wanted, we would trim off any branches they requested.

The next step was carrying the tree over to the person's car and using twine to secure the tree to the top of the car. Each worker had little variations on this method, but we were all taught by the owner of the company how to secure a tree to various vehicles.

When the lot was busy, it was a whirlwind of grabbing trees, making the cuts, and tying them to the roof of cars. We sold almost 800 trees. On our busiest day, we sold 51 trees. That is a little over 4 trees an hour.

During slow periods of the day, one of us would go into the RV to prepare lunch or grab some drinks and snacks. We'd also give our dog a break to go potty and walk around a bit.

Whenever business died down, the entire crew would help re-fill the empty cups with trees from the back. At about 8:45 PM, I would start putting tools away, closing things up, and turn-ing off lights. Natalie would fill out the paperwork with the counts of the day and make sure she had the right amount of cash. Once the lights were turned off, we ate dinner, showered, and collapsed into bed. That was the basic schedule seven days a week for about a month and a half.

Holiday Decorators

Christmas Decor of Knoxville, as its name clearly notes, specializes in holiday decorations. The company decorates business fronts and residential properties with mostly outdoor lighting on roofs and trees. With some clients, specialty decorations like garland, wreaths, giant Christmas trees, and nativity scenes are assembled and displayed. With its ever-growing clientele, this Knoxville business begins its season October 1st and stretches into the first one or two weeks of February. A season consists of two parts, "install" and "takedown."

The "install" portion of Christmas Decor runs from October to December, typically the beginning of October to the first or second week of December. ("Takedown" is from the beginning of January to the first or second week of February.) As installers, our job was to display lights on roofs, trees, and bushes. Garland and wreaths were hung from doorways, windows, and balconies. Equipment like ladders, lifts, poles, and harnesses was used to reach higher places.

You have your pick, depending on comfort and skill level, whether you want to work on roofs or remain a member of the ground crew. One thing is for certain, you should not be afraid of heights in this job because climbing ladders is a guarantee. For the most part, we installed lights at several companies and homes in and around Knoxville. I was a roofer, and Natalie was a part of the ground crew.

We worked an average of 12 hours a day during setup, but it wasn't unusual to work more than that. Spending that many hours a day on a roof, tree, or ladder could be punishing on the body. We frequently had sore feet, arms, and legs. Tylenol and Ibuprofen became our best friend.

We both loved viewing the locations at night and seeing our handiwork on display! The customers were very complimentary, and we later learned that many installments were purchased as gifts or surprises for family and friends.

The takedown portion of the season was completed in half the time and what felt like half the effort. The process is the reverse of the installment. We were undoing lights and decorations and storing them in their proper bins. Unlike install, takedown consisted of 8-hour days, no overtime. Frigid weather with below-freezing temperatures was more prevalent during the latter half of the season, so it was imperative to dress in layers.

As far as benefits, starting pay was $12 per hour with opportunities for a bump in pay throughout the season. Roofers started at $13 per hour. Time and a half was paid after 40 hours each week. A bonus was rewarded for completing the full season (install and takedown), and an additional bonus was paid to returning workers.

We stayed at an RV park a mere mile or two from the warehouse, our meeting place every morning. We were responsible for monthly rent, which was about $350. Electricity was a separate charge.

A Day in The Life of...

Our RV park was only about a couple miles from the company building/shop. During set up, we would get to the shop and clock in. Team leaders would be ready with a small pile of paperwork, each sheet detailing the assignment location, specifics on types and amount of lights, garland, and/or wreaths, and a picture of design layout.

The rest of the workers would be split up into teams based on the size of the job(s). Some days that meant taking several vehicles to one location, and other days there were several teams of four or five at various homes and businesses.

Once supplies were packed up in the company trucks, we would head out to the job sites. If the job included roof lights, a roofer or two would be on the team. Returning customers already had roof lights custom fit to their buildings or homes. Each string of lights would have a tag with a diagram showing where the string of lights started and ended. If the roof was for a new customer, the roofers got busy cutting and splicing the light strands to fit that roof.

It may sound complicated, but at the beginning of each season, there is a training session explaining how to cut and splice wires. Typically no previous experience is necessary. The only prequalification for a roofer is you can't be afraid of heights.

Roofs are not easy things to walk on, and some required me to move rather slowly even with a safety harness on. For that reason, the ground crew usually completed tasks faster than the roofing crew. If you decide to be a roofer, plan on walking on steep inclines of roofs for at least eight to ten hours a day.

While I was on a roof all day, the majority of Natalie's day was spent on ladders of various types (e.g., step, orchard, and extension ladders) and heights (ranging from 6 to 24 feet). As a ground crew member, she wrapped light strings around bushes and tree branches and put wreaths and garland around doorways, mailboxes, and balconies.

The paperwork for each assignment stipulated which doors, windows, or balconies had garland or wreaths. It designated which trees and bushes were wrapped and the method of wrapping. A tree was decorated by using large bulbs wrapped around its canopy and trunk, or each branch was wrapped with mini lights.

The paperwork also noted the number of lights to use for each tree. Knowing exactly how many lights were put in each decoration was extremely important because we had to avoid burning out lights or tripping breakers.

The ground crew, more so than the roofing crew, had to be able to think critically and creatively about how to make the decorations pop! In other words, they always had to have their inner Martha Stewart with them.

We packed our own lunches, and on the rare occasion, grabbed a meal from a fast-food joint. Bathrooms were nonexistent at most sites, so we would make sure to stop at gas stations and use the restrooms in between jobs. At the end of the day, we would get back to the shop and take out any remaining supplies we didn't use.

*****

The takedown or final portion of the season was basically the same as the setup process, with a few exceptions. All the roof lights had to be taken off, coiled up, and tagged. The garland had to be taken down, unhooked, and flattened out for better storage. The mini-lights were unwrapped from the trees and rolled up into balls before being stacked into tubs.

"FILLER JOBS"

When it comes to the span of workamping jobs, there is no clear-cut duration. On our end, most of our seasonal assignments last from 4-6 months. There are, however, plenty of short-term gigs that are available throughout the year, crossing various seasons, that ask for a mere week to month commitment. We have dubbed these "filler jobs."

Just like any other seasonal position, benefits vary with filler jobs. Some employers may offer a full hookup site in exchange for an agreed-upon number of hours worked per traveler, or you may see the opposite side of the coin, all hours paid including free site.

Until recently, we did not have the availability on our schedule to take on a filler job. We have heard or read other workamper accounts about their involvement with Nascar race weekends, Renaissance festivals, Major League Baseball spring training, and the Houston Livestock Show and Rodeo.

After full-time RVing for a couple of years, we started to feel a slight disconnect from communities. We decided to fill this void by volunteering. We looked at a whole host of possibilities. Habitat for Humanity reaches out to RVers to assist with home construction and renovation projects across the nation. Lighthouse hosts are asked to commit at least a month to run the visitor's center or give tours. The U.S. Fish and Wildlife Service always needs extra hands to continue various tasks like monitoring wildlife populations, habitat cleanups, and help build awareness of certain causes through community activities.

We are big animal lovers and decided upon an animal sanctuary as our first filler job.

Safe Harbor Farm Volunteering

We spent a couple of weeks volunteering at Safe Harbor Farm in Maysville, North Carolina. Safe Harbor Farm (SHF, for short) is an animal sanctuary that once housed 75 cats, up to 40 dogs, 12 goats, and over 10 birds. Now it consists of about a dozen cats, 6 dogs. 4 goats, 1 turkey vulture, 1 duck, lots of turtles and other assorted wildlife. They are listed as an official turtle sanctuary. The organization doesn't do quite the volume of the physical rescue of dogs as they have in the past. SHF has always been focused on dog behavior education to reduce the number of dogs returned to shelters around the country.

As volunteer workampers, our agreement was to put in 16 hours per week, per person, completing a variety of projects, mostly outside work. This included projects like raking and clearing brush, mowing, repairing fences, and placing logs around the property pond for turtles to sunbathe. We also helped during feeding time. For these efforts, we received a full hookup site on the property and the use of the laundry facility.

When we first got the idea to workamp seasonal jobs, we had no idea that there were so many jobs out there. There are plenty of jobs we have not experienced and want to try out. Now that you have an idea of different types of seasonal jobs, you may be wondering where you can look to find these jobs. Once you find a job you want, how do you apply for it, and what should you expect from the application process? The next section will answer just that.

SECTION THREE:

*How We Find Jobs and the
Application Process*

WHERE TO LOOK FOR SEASONAL WORKAMPING JOBS

Online

There are a number of ways to find seasonal workamping jobs. The quickest, most straight-forward method would be to look online. A general search on "workamping jobs" will produce a list of websites that dedicate much of their content towards this cause. With these many organizations, RVers can find all types of seasonal employment in the form of work ads. These ads include information on the company, job roles, location, duration of employment, compensation benefits, and contact information. The ad may also include specifications on what to send (e.g., resume, picture of rig) if interested in applying for or getting more information on the job.

The following are popular workamping websites seasonal and full-time RVers often visit. Most of the options offer free subscriptions. There are a few, however, that may require some sort of annual fee to access job listings or additional services related to job application. Additional subscription fees will be mentioned in the description if it applies.

Workamper News
workamper.com/

Workamper News advertises work ads online daily via their "Hotline Jobs" page and through their bi-monthly magazine. Their classifieds list hundreds of temporary and long-term opportunities with businesses around the country. They advertise any kind of workamping job you can think of in places like campgrounds, amusement parks, oil fields, wineries, holiday lots,

Amazon, and everywhere in between.

They have several membership levels starting from $0. The free membership option provides access to job ads; however, they are delayed, giving paid members first access. The three levels of paid membership, starting at around $20 per year, come with an array of tools that enhance the application experience including a resume builder, the ability to run a personal work wanted ad, discounts to organization rallies and webinars, and more.

CoolWorks
CoolWorks.com

CoolWorks lists jobs in top tourist destinations like ski resorts, national parks, dude ranches and beachfront resorts. The beauty of these seasonal opportunities is not so much the monetary compensation but the location itself. Being able to live and work in what many consider "dream destinations" is the main benefit.

Keeping this in the forefront, compensation can be volunteer-based or hourly payment, with or without an RV site provided. In some situations, on site lodging is the only option for workers. Ads are organized online by job description, season, location, and there is even a section specifically for jobs that come with an RV site. CoolWorks is free to use and no subscription is needed.

PeakSeason
peakseason.com/

PeakSeason is a site that is similar to CoolWorks but mainly lists jobs in mountain towns and resort destinations.

Workers on Wheels
work-for-rvers-and-campers.com

Workers on Wheels was created in the 90s by an RVing

couple, Bob and Coleen. They are respected in the RV community and have been making a living on the road for well over two decades, going on three. Bob and Coleen feature job listings, RV living tips, workamper experiences, and travel stories in their weekly newsletters. It takes some time to poke around and read through the site's plethora of information, but it is worth taking the time to look through.

Similar sites to Workers on Wheels that list workamping opportunities are happyvagabonds.com, workingcouples.com, and workampingjobs.com.

Kampgrounds of America
workatkoa.com/

Kampgrounds of America, KOA for short, can be found in over 500 places in the United States and neighboring Canada. The campground chain has been around for over fifty years. In that time, they have relied on workampers to keep their operations running smoothly from year to year and season to season. In order to access employment ads from virtually all KOA facilities, it is necessary to obtain annual club membership which starts at $35 per year.

You can complete an online resume through workatkoa.com. Many workampers only seek employment with KOA campgrounds. The transition from one location to the next is a smoother, seamless experience within the KOA corporation since all campgrounds use the same reservation software system, run similar camp programs and activities, and enforce comparable rules and regulations.

American Land and Leisure
americanll.com

American Land and Leisure is a private contractor that regularly places workampers in campgrounds located on federal lands in many states. If you're looking for a job that is away from it all, their site may be a good place to look.

Volunteer.gov
volunteer.gov/

Volunteer.gov lists volunteer positions that help maintain and restore our country's land and natural resources. They offer positions at campgrounds, lighthouses, beaches, visitor centers, and nature sanctuaries. If you ever wanted to help agencies like the U.S. Army Corps of Engineers, National Park Service, Fish and Wildlife Service, Forest Service, and Bureau of Land Management, check out their site to see if you can give back to the country.

Habitat for Humanity
habitat.org/volunteer/travel-and-build/rv-care-a-vanners

This global organization reaches out to RVers as well. There are many construction projects scheduled throughout the year in states across the nation. RVers typically spend two weeks, 7 days a week helping with different stages of construction or renovation on designated homes. Prior experience is not a requirement, and task-specific training is provided at each work site. RV parking near the construction site is arranged in advance and either free of charge or available at a reduced price.

Popular Seasonal Workamping Gigs

We went into detail about our experiences with the sugar beet harvest and Amazon CamperForce, so it would only make sense to include a direct link to access further details on the programs, along with application procedures. Information on the sugar beet harvest we participated in can be gathered here, theunbeetableexperience.com. Updates on Amazon Camper-Force can be read here, amazondelivers.jobs/about/camperforce/.

Word of Mouth and Brochures

Good old-fashioned word of mouth is a perfect way to find jobs. We have found some jobs this way. It's a good idea to tuck away any information fellow workampers give you for later job searches.

While we were workamping at an RV park in Michigan, a fellow workamper told us about a holiday job he went back to every year. He told us about his experience setting up Christmas lights on houses and the abundance of overtime pay. He gave us the company card with contact information. We held onto the card, not intending to look into it that year.

Another couple in the same park told us all about a mom-and-pop company that hired folks to manage their collection of Christmas tree lots. The couple absolutely loved their experience and encouraged us to look into it. Again, we filed their recommendation away.

Eventually, when the time was right, we contacted both places, mentioning our referring co-workers and were offered jobs. We ended up returning to one of the jobs for a second season.

On a different note, we know a couple who has found several workamping jobs by browsing the travel brochures in visitor centers. Many brochures advertise tourist places that need extra help during their busy seasons. They simply use the contact information in the brochure to inquire about jobs.

Make Your Own Way

For the most part, we have shared the same workamping jobs with similar roles and similar schedules. Although we have enjoyed working together these years, we decided to change things up one summer. I took a detour and looked for a seasonal job on indeed.com.

I am a certified Scuba Instructor, so I decided on a whim to search the entire US for scuba diving jobs. I came across an ad for a company called Waterfront Restoration near Minneapolis that hired scuba divers for the summer season to pull weeds.

There was, of course, a couple of hang-ups with the position. The first was that an RV site was not included, so we would need to pay for a site. The second issue was that I would have a job, and Natalie would not.

Natalie got right to job hunting and started calling up RV parks, inquiring about summer help. Fortunately, there was a KOA about 20 miles south of Waterfront's office that was hiring workampers. She applied and got the job before I even heard back from Waterfront for an interview. The KOA offered her a position with an hourly wage and an RV site at a drastically reduced monthly fee.

I was finally contacted and hired by Waterfront Restoration. As a bonus, I ended up certifying many of their new employees as divers. I was able to handle the classes as an independent instructor and charge the students directly. I also ended up working part-time at the KOA to help get the park ready to open when we first arrived.

There are no set rules when looking at workamping options. It is possible to create a workamping scenario from various sources to fit your wants and needs. You don't always have to work the same job as your traveling partner, and you don't always have to look at workamper specific sites to find them.

WHEN TO START YOUR JOB SEARCH

Since most of our income is derived from seasonal workamping employment, we tend to start searching for jobs and filling out applications anywhere from 4 months to a year in advance of the job's start date. This way, we can set up and secure one seasonal job after the next for sometimes an entire year. Having a pre-arranged work schedule gives a little peace of mind knowing that the job search task is done and out of the way for a while.

Some RVers like this depth of planning, knowing where they are going and what they are doing for months to come. Others feel just as comfortable planning as they go. They may read or hear about a job needing immediate help and jump on the opportunity.

Keep in mind that employers have their own timelines regarding reviewing and accepting applications. Corporations like Amazon CamperForce and Express Employment with the sugar beet harvest begin their application and hiring process well in advance of the actual start dates in the fall. Workampers should expect to apply at the beginning of the year, January thru April.

Workampers looking to find summer jobs can start applying up to a year in advance. However, many summer assignments are posted at the end of winter/beginning of spring. It is common to see work ads posted anytime businesses see a sharp increase in service demands. This happens if the employer underestimated the number of staff members needed, or employees left the company for one reason or another.

Not long into our workamping career, we realized it was

possible to get a job any time of the year. We don't always have to plan months ahead to know we have options, especially during the summer months.

WHAT TO CONSIDER WHEN LOOKING FOR A JOB

Each workamper has his/her own preferences. When we are looking for workamping jobs, we are checking off three major categories: compensation, location, and experience. First, we look at the practical aspects of the job. As mentioned several times, we are non-retired RVers and rely on seasonal workamping jobs to bring in the bulk of our monthly funds. With this in mind, we look for work that offers all or most hours paid and provides a free or drastically discounted full hookup RV site.

Location is another factor. We look for places in North America that we have not yet explored and would like to explore. This isn't always realistic, but we make it work the best we can. In the first couple of years, we traveled hundreds, sometimes thousands of miles between jobs. Although we love road trips and traveling, we found that the travel days and wear and tear on the RV were not so great. We have since tried to keep seasonal jobs relatively within the same region to not only decrease mileage but also allow for more time to really get to know an area and all its treasures.

Above everything, though, we like to try new things when it comes to choosing the next job. Part of the fun of exploring new places is experiencing different manners of labor and helping within a community. Never in our wildest imaginations did we think that we would be behind the production lines of an Amazon warehouse, arranging holiday lights on the longest pedestrian suspension bridge in Gatlinburg, operating a piling machine in the wee hours of the morning while sugar beets shoot out into a 25-foot pile, displaying hundreds of pumpkins and Christmas trees for purchase, or serving one sample of wine after another to hundreds of bikers during a Sturgis Rally in South Dakota. We leave every new workamping experience with a broader skill set and a newfound appreciation for workers in these contrasting fields.

Of course, how we choose the next job is not necessarily the same for others. There are several factors to consider when looking for your next workamping job. In no particular order, the following are aspects of a seasonal job to ponder during the decision-making process. If you are not a solo traveler, it is important to take each factor into consideration with your traveling partner and/or family and ultimately come to a consensus.

Labor vs. Compensation

RVers decide to take on seasonal workamping jobs for an assortment of reasons. They enjoy the break in travel, want the experience of meeting people and new locations, feel the drive to contribute to a company or cause, and/or need funds. Regardless of the reason, as a seasonal workamper, your services to any organization are valuable and should have equal compensation value.

Are the job responsibilities and hours a fair trade for the proposed pay and/or barter exchange? Whether we choose a volunteer or paid position, one of the aspects of a job we look at is the labor versus compensation agreement.

Compensation can come in the form of hourly wage or salary, end of the season completion bonus, partial or full hookup RV site or on-site living arrangements at a discount or free of charge, access to business amenities (e.g., laundry use, pool access, free miniature golf play), business store discounts, and/or free or discounted admission to local attractions.

Monetary compensation, for us, is a given. If the total monthly gain meets or exceeds our monthly budget, that job is a high possibility. We also look at the living arrangements. Free full hookup site is a green light, but more thought and review is allotted for cases where the employer requests payment for the site and/or utilities. They may trade cash or a certain number of hours worked for the site. We research the site costs and determine if the payment requested is excessive or matches its value. Extra incentives like all access or discounted admission to local attractions or company amenities can sweeten the pot and save us a lot of money we would otherwise be paying to enjoy.

Location

Searching for the next location to work is perhaps the most enjoyable part of the job hunt. Seasonal workamping can take RVers to remote, mountainous getaways, smack dab in the middle of a Midwest campground, or along a coastal paradise. Some workampers strategically map out their route, paying close attention to the weather, the distance between jobs, and access to the best attractions. Others close their eyes and aim a dart at a map.

Some location features to think about include climate, probable weather extremes, and the distance of the RV site from the worksite and from essential resources like food and supplies. Some workamping locations are chosen because they are close to extended family members or near medical offices if regular health visits are needed.

Besides the ever-changing landscape, another constant change in our workamping experiences has been with varying climates. We've workamped in locations with extreme climates: Las Vegas summer heat and Midwest winter freeze. Those opportunities have helped us figure out how to set up our rig for better insulation and moisture control. It is possible to live and work comfortably in varying conditions. We learned to keep our location options open because of this.

Interest in Job Assignment

Seasonal, temporary workamping jobs are diverse. RVers can work familiar jobs or find completely new experiences. The latter is the route we typically choose.

Initially, while researching the concept of workamping, we didn't think working jobs out of our skill set was even possible. In fact, we worried that we wouldn't be hired to work at a campground. We had no background experience with this industry. We learned two things very quickly.

First, we learned that we could always apply our previous (pre-full-time RVing) work experience to any seasonal workamping job in some capacity. Some of the most basic and key qualifications of a good employee are reliability, punctuality, commitment to performance, and good communication.

These are baseline skills that can be referenced with practically any prior job experiences. If you can show examples of these attributes in a resume and/or during the interview process, this will convey loads to an employer. On top of this, we've learned over the years that employers are looking for applicants that are eager to learn new skills, take action, and are flexible.

Secondly, more often than not, seasonal jobs welcome new, inexperienced applicants, and they will openly mention this in their work ads. In these cases, some degree of training or certification is offered. If training is not obviously mentioned in the work ad, we make sure to ask when we email or call up the company.

Length of Commitment

Natalie and I joke, saying that we usually get the itch to take off to the next place or job after three months of staying put. Seasonal jobs vary in length of commitment. As we have mentioned with the jobs we have already worked, employment can be a mere week or two to year-round. On average, our assignments last 4 months.

Employers rely on their workampers to complete the term of their assignment. As an incentive, some companies offer an end-of-season bonus. We make every effort to complete our contracted assignment, not only because it speaks volumes when you keep a commitment, but we don't want to burn any bridges. We also make sure that our separate seasonal commitments don't cross timelines, essentially that we don't double book jobs.

Employee Reviews

How often have you sought a second opinion? When researching potential jobs, we will seek other workamper opinions and reviews on their experiences with a company. There have been many situations where we can ask someone face-to-face, especially if it is a co-worker that is recommending a particular gig.

Many workampers have blogs or vlogs where they document their experience and personal take on a job. Facebook groups and various online forums are other sources. If you opted for a paid membership with Workampers News, subscribers have access to workamper reviews. We don't solely base our final decision on these reviews, but we take them into consideration.

BUILDING YOUR WORKAMPER RESUME AND APPLYING FOR A JOB

We have applied for most of our seasonal workamping jobs online, either by an employer's website or by emailing a resume. It's rare but we have gotten one or two jobs by simply calling the employer and coming to an agreement over the phone. Each job ad will give specific instructions on what to send and how to apply.

One thing we learned early on with job ads is to read them carefully and send in what is requested. Employers ask for these items for a reason, and failing to send in an item may mean that your information is discarded first. Many of our previous employers have often overlooked applicants if they do not send in all parts stipulated in the ad.

Some ads might ask for photos of you and your rig along with your resume. We've noticed this request from campgrounds and resorts. This is mostly to give the park a face to associate with a name, and they want to make sure your RV doesn't look like it's going to collapse in on itself. Keep in mind you and your RV will be affiliated with the campground while you work and live there.

Building a Workamper Resume

Before you can apply for a job, you need a resume that gives deserved credit to your many talents and work experience. It needs to set you apart from other workamping applicants. It seems like a daunting task, but it can be as simple as making a few tweaks to your existing resume. These adjustments might mean rearranging content to emphasize your capabilities and adding more detailed descriptions to better match job responsibilities.

There are many ways and many opinions about how to format a resume. In no reflection of the word do we think that we are "experts" in the subject matter, however, we have some insight on what has worked from firsthand experience. Consider our organization and content first, and then pick and choose what components will work in your own resume.

We divide our resume into four general categories: personal information, education, special skills, and work experience. Each category is described below, and some have accompanying excerpts from my resume as examples.

Personal Information

The first part of a resume should give the employer your name, address, email, and phone number. After all, you want the employer to be able to contact you easily. This portion fits into the heading of our document. An example of what our header looks like can be seen below.

John Doe

123 Rainbow Drive #1234
Livingston, TX 77399
555-555-5555
johndoe@mail.com

Education

The word "Education" in bold immediately follows my personal information section. If you have a college degree, trade school, or specialty training related to the workamping position, you can include it here. If you don't have anything of note to put here, this section is not required.

To be perfectly honest, I have come across very few, if any, workamping jobs that require a college degree. In many cases my degree doesn't relate to the job. So why would I place this section first after our contact information? We feel this section is important because it not only gives the employer information on our educational background, but it also gives a sense of our dedication and drive, sticking with something to the end.

EDUCATION

Associates of Applied Science in Photography with an emphasis in Video and Film Community College of Southern Nevada, Las Vegas, Nevada
August 2009

Special Skills

Whether you are new to workamping or going into your third year as a seasonal employee, this might be a section of your resume to include next before delving into your work experience. The purpose of this portion is to immediately list skills relevant to the job. After perusing the work ad, I find specific examples of skills I possess that align with the job description.

Some special skills I have included on my resume are customer service, computer skills, home repair, landscaping, and even scuba diving experience (if appropriate). Depending on the skill, I'll make sure to specify any particular equipment and tools used, programs operated, certifications or training earned, and length of experience. These categories are rearranged, added, or deleted based on the job I am applying for.

For example, let's say I was a new workamper, and I was applying for an outside camp host position. The job ad specified a camp host couple with strong customer service skills. One person would be working outside/maintenance while the other worked in the office. I would need to show the employer in my resume that I possessed the skills to work in maintenance and have good customer service. Below is an example of how I would convey that information.

HOME REPAIR EXPERIENCE

- 5+ years of experience owning, maintaining and remodeling my own home
- Maintained a half acre grass front yard to homeowner association's specifications
- Repaired common plumbing problems such as replacing sinks and troubleshooting toilets
- Repaired minor electrical problems such as changing electrical sockets and tripped breakers
- Replaced over 1,800 square feet of carpet with laminate flooring

CUSTOMER SERVICE EXPERIENCE

- Worked as a tour guide for groups as large as 50 customers for over 5 years
- 10+ years of retail experience
- Owned my own business in the service industry taking care of customer's pets
- Worked as a tech specialist for a company that handled silent auctions at high dollar fundraising events

Starting with the first part of the example above, I don't have any professional maintenance experience to list. I do, however, have a bit of experience working on my own house. I am pretty competent mowing lawns, can troubleshoot minor problems, and I knew enough about construction to lay laminate flooring, all of which are valuable skills for an RV park maintenance position. It's perfectly fine to draw from pretty much all of your life skills, professionally or not, to show an employer that you are qualified for a job or at least possess a little background knowledge in the area.

In most workamping jobs, we have found that the employer isn't expecting you to be an expert mechanic or know their reservation software already. They just want to feel you are capable and willing to learn the job with the skill set you do possess. When you see a job that asks for skills in industries you haven't necessarily worked in, think about hobbies and life experiences outside of work that may match those skills and make sure to add them to the "Special Skills" part of your resume.

In contrast, for the strong customer service skill the employer was looking for, I pulled from my professional experience. Granted, as the employer looked into my work history, they would have seen all of the jobs I listed there. However, by compiling those specific jobs into the "Special Skills" section, I highlighted that experience right away, saving the employer from having to hunt for it.

Work Experience

After describing relevant skills, I jump into the final part of the resume. My "Work Experience" starts with my most recent job. For each job, I'll list my position title, company name and location, and record the dates of my employment. Then I list the numerous tasks performed while in that position, regardless if they were minute or repetitive. Below is an example of what my "Work Experience" section looked like when we applied to our first workamping job.

WORK EXPERIENCE

Tour Guide (LE REVE)
EBG, Las Vegas
December 2013 to January 2014
www.entertainmentbenefits.com
    Gave a backstage tour of LE REVE at the Wynn for up to 25 people; maintained control and safety of the guests while giving them a VIP experience

Open Water Scuba Instructor
Scuba Views, Las Vegas

June 2012 to January 2014
www.scubaviews.com
> Assisted the dive instructor in training students how to dive; led dives for certified divers using safe diving practices; performed normal retail shop duties: cashier, stocker, custodian; serviced and cleaned rental dive equipment; inspected SCUBA tanks according to Department of Transportation standards; assisted customers with making informed decisions on equipment purchases; rebuilt and maintained the www.scubaviews.com website

How far back should you go with work history? The standard is somewhere between 10 to 15 years according to most job building and resume sites I have found. Workamping jobs can add up pretty quickly though. We found that many employers seem to be most interested in our previous workamping jobs now that we have quite a few under our belt. It is for that reason, we started separating our workamping experience from all our other work experiences. As an example, below is what my resume looked like after completing my first workamping job.

WORK CAMPING EXPERIENCE

Camp Host
Desert Rose RV Park
Fernley, NV
June 2015 to October 2015
> Performed routine duties for outside maintenance; escorted campers to their sites, maintained lawn, cleaned bathhouse and rec room, pulled weeds, repaired minor electrical problems, handled customer concerns while exhibiting great customer service.

OTHER WORK EXPERIENCE

Tour Guide (LE REVE)
EBG, Las Vegas
December 2013 to January 2014
www.entertainmentbenefits.com

Gave a backstage tour of LE REVE at the Wynn for up to 25 people; maintained control and safety of the guests while giving them a VIP experience

Open Water Scuba Instructor
Scuba Views, Las Vegas
June 2012 to January 2014
www.scubaviews.com

Assisted the dive instructor in training students how to dive; led dives for certified divers using safe diving practices; performed normal retail shop duties: cashier, stocker, custodian; serviced and cleaned rental dive equipment; inspected SCUBA tanks according to Department of Transportation standards; assisted customers with making informed decisions on equipment purchases; rebuilt and maintained the www.scubaviews.com website

Online Application

Once you have built or updated your resume it's time to apply for a workamping job. You are most likely to run into an online application for large companies like Amazon, the sugar beet harvest, and national parks. These online applications are usually very standard and walk you through the process of inputting your information. Sometimes they will have an option to upload your resume as well.

Take Amazon CamperForce, for example, which requires filling out an online application and then attaching a copy of your high school diploma. The online application process was pretty cut-and-dry asking for basic information: name and address, education and work history, and task, shift, and facility preferences. A personality assessment ended the application. Express Employment (with the beet harvest) mirrored Amazon's application minus a diploma copy and personality assessment.

Natalie and I usually have to fill out online applications separately. There has been an entry in some applications asking for the name of your travel partner, especially if both parties are applying. Amazon's application process asks each applicant to put the name of their traveling partner so they can associate the two together.

Emailing Your Resume

If Natalie and I are both applying to the same business, we will combine our resumes and photos of us and our rig into one file. By combine, I mean, the file contains my complete resume, her complete resume, and photos at the end of the document. It's ok if both of your resumes aren't formatted exactly the same way; ours aren't.

We use the initial email to the employer as the cover letter, taking an opportunity to briefly introduce ourselves, before explaining that our resumes and any other requested information is attached. Other workampers prefer to include a cover with the resume/photo package. This is a personal preference.

Adding a Cover Letter

The cover letter is a virtual handshake to the company. It is our introduction, peppered with a bit of our personalities. Examples of prior work experience are mentioned. We talk about why we are interested in applying for the job and wanting to learn more about the unique opportunity. We express our excitement about hearing back from the company and make sure to attach a copy of our resumes along with any other pieces requested in the work ad.

Over the years, our cover letter has evolved. You'll notice this after reading our *New* and *Seasoned Workamper* examples. Because we had zero experience as workampers, we fell back on our talents, skills and professional background to accentuate our capabilities, education, and past employment.

Example Cover Letter (New Workamper)

Hello!

My name is Natalie. My husband, Levi, and I will be full-time RVers starting this summer of 2015. We are responding to a job ad you put in Workamper News magazine. We are very interested in working at your RV park and can start as early as June.

Levi is Mr. Jack-of-All-Trades and has made a living in the fields of entertainment (acting, performing magic and comedy), graphic and web design, retail/sales, videography, photography, scuba diving (instructor and commercial), animal care, computer repair/troubleshooting, and general home repair. He has 15+ years of experience working with the public and providing customer service.

I have spent over a decade working in the fields of childcare and education (with students ranging from ages 3 to 12, diagnosed with special needs). I co-owned a pet sitting business with Levi. My experience in the classroom and customer service has given me great problem-solving skills, and I keep going until the job is done.

Though we are new to working in RV parks and workamping in general, we are both willing and able to learn and have a strong work ethic. We have included a copy of our resumes along with a picture of us and our 26 foot, 2011 Itasca. We look forward to your response!

Sincerely,

Natalie and Levi Henley
Natalie's cell 555-555-5555
Levi's cell 555-555-5555

After five years of workamping, we have started listing our assortment of jobs in the cover letter. By mentioning all these contrasting positions, we want to convey that not only are we flexible and willing to work in a variety of settings, but we have experience in many job fields.

We make sure to include or separately note if we have prior work experience with the position we are seeking. For the employer, a candidate with more experience does not need as much time and effort to train and prepare for a familiar job.

Example Cover Letter (Seasoned Workapmer)

Hello!

My name is Natalie! My husband, Levi, and I are full-time RVers. We travel all over he country and workamp in various states. We have worked as camp hosts, Amazon CamperForce associates, sugar beet harvest employees, wine tasting associates, holiday decorators, classroom teacher, scuba instructor, magician, bloggers, and magazine feature writers, to name a few.

We came across your work ad in the latest Workamper News magazine and are interested in joining the summer 2020 workamping team! We are particularly interested in your posted openings with maintenance, campground activities, and front desk. We feel that our work camping experiences, combined with our excellent work ethics, will be a great fit for the company!

We have included a copy of our resumes along with a picture of us and our

26 foot 2011 Itasca. Our website henleyshappytrails.com details our adventures on the road and past work camping experiences. We look forward to your response, and thank you for your time and consideration as additions to (business name)!

Sincerely,

Natalie and Levi Henley
Natalie's cell 555-555-5555
Levi's cell 555-555-5555

Remember that the purpose of the cover letter is to get the employer to read your resume. The cover letter should be short, sweet, and to the point. It shouldn't go more than one page long.

Letters of Recommendation and References

Besides a resume, some companies may request letters of recommendation or references. For convenience sake, collect letters of reference before completing a job assignment. This avoids having to track down someone to write a letter and then wait to receive it. This time factor could be the one item delaying an application process.

If the company does not specify information to include regarding references, we typically tack on three to the end of our resume. Our list is comprised of supervisors and co-workers. When contacted, we want our references to give varying viewpoints of our work habits, some overseeing our production and others working alongside us on a daily basis. Along with each name we include his/her job title, phone number, and email address. We make sure to get their consent before including them on this list.

Regardless of what it requested in the application process, whether it is an application or a resume with all the bells and whistles of a cover letter and references, proofread everything! Make sure all sections that need to be completed in an application are filled out. Double check that little things like dates of employment are accurate. Check for any spelling or grammar errors in the cover letter and make sure that the contact information for each reference is listed correctly.

The resume and/or application is quite possibly the most important of the application process. Consider them the meat of your sandwich. The interview process is your bread, supporting your work experience and skill sets. Any follow up after the interview is the cheese and sauce, adding a little extra flavor to the already delectable creation.

Final Note

Most companies send some sort of confirmation email telling us they received our initial application or resume. If we don't hear back from them, we send a follow-up email to make sure they received it. We wait at least a week or two before doing this in order to give them a chance to respond.

PREPARING FOR THE INTERVIEW

For the purposes of this section and with the understanding that not all seasonal workamping positions will include an interview process, we will set aside large corporations like Amazon and the sugar beet harvest. Our focus here is with businesses that utilize some form of an interview as part of their hiring procedures.

As part of the hiring process, many employers opt to call or video chat with potential employees, knowing that they will be miles away at the time exploring countrysides or workamping elsewhere. These interviews are crucial, not only for the employer attempting to find the right individual for the job but for the applicant searching for the right mixture of preferred job benefits, location, and responsibilities.

In preparation for an interview, we always confirm the date and time of the interview, making sure to verify time zones. We clear our schedule on the day of the interview and select a quiet location with good reception to take the call. If our only option is in a busy RV park, we may even post a note outside of our door, letting everyone know that we'll be unavailable during this time.

We generally set up a few items in front of us to use and reference during the interview as well. This includes a list of questions, work ad, our resumes, and something to jot down notes. Depending on the type of call, we will set up our area, our phone or laptop, 10-15 minutes in advance, and wait for the call.

A Side Note

First impressions speak volumes, and having a purpose and direction coming into the interview shows not only your interest in the job but also your desire to put your best foot forward. This is why we come prepared with background information about the company and job roles. We make sure to do some research, usually online through the company's website and customer reviews, so we know a bit of the back story on how the company started, their notable aspects, and what the surrounding location has to offer. We'll also have a list of questions regarding company attributes as a way of showing not only interest but the fact that we put some time and effort into learning about their establishment. We did our homework, and we want the potential employer to know this.

Our past interviews have usually begun with greetings and small talk about our current location and activities. Since we have already sent our cover letter and resume, the employer or hiring department representative usually has a general grasp of our work history and skill sets. They may, however, take this initial time to clarify certain items mentioned in the resume, like the level of experience within a job field. We've been asked about our desire to incorporate our expertise, not specific to the job we are applying for, with other or additional responsibilities in the company.

For example, Natalie was originally assigned an office/receptionist position at a campground. During the phone interview, the owner of the park noticed that she was an elementary teacher for over a decade and asked if she'd mind organizing and running the campground activities too.

A little advice if you are new to a job assignment...

If you are new to workamping, let the employer know. I know we have mentioned it already, but it bears repeating. Most workamping employers are less interested in whether you already know how to do the job and more interested in your willingness to learn.

For example, our fourth workamping job was at an RV park in

Michigan. During the phone interview, I was told that the outside crew worked on cabin roofs, put in drainage ditches, and did all of the landscaping. The park even had a full-on woodshop. I had no idea how to do half of the tasks mentioned.

Without coming out and saying, "I can't do any of that," I asked if they had a staff of knowledgeable people that would show me how to do the tasks mentioned. The interviewer assured me that I would be assisting people who knew what they were doing, and they would help me with any unfamiliar tasks.

We have been asked an assortment of questions by the interviewers. Why are you interested in working with our company? What kind of experience do you have regarding (insert skill: customer service, maintenance, retail, etc.)?

Situational questions were posed during our interview with Prairie Berry. For instance, since the job of the wine tasting associate required us to engage in conversation with the guests while talking about the history of the winery and aspects of each wine sample, we were each asked to recall a funny story about ourselves. The purpose of this, the hiring duo later explained, was to get an idea of our storytelling capabilities along with our ability to capture the audience's attention.

Still, other interviews have been simple, straightforward questions. When are you available to begin work? Are you ok with working varying shifts but still have the same days off? Do you have any problems working with cats? Yes, we were asked that last question while interviewing for a campground. The owner had two cats that lived in the park office.

We have had some interviews where we are the only party asking questions. These are usually the less stress-inducing calls because we feel in control of the conversation, steering it with our questions and concerns.

Because every RVer has their own expectations when they

choose to workamp, it is vital that they get all the information they can before agreeing to a job offer. Over the course of the years, after several phone interviews, we were able to develop a list of questions to help determine if a job was the right match for our wants and needs.

Most of our seasonal jobs that included interviews as part of the hiring process were campground jobs. Some of the questions below reflect these types of assignments. Although some of these questions may not be pertinent to your prospective job(s), they may help in the development of your own list of questions. If any answers to our questions were mentioned in the company's job description/post, we still asked them (e.g., job description, use of an RV site) just to verify that information was still up to date. The questions are in no particular order.

What are the responsibilities associated with the position(s)?

How are we compensated for hours worked? Full hookup (FHU) site? Payment for hours worked?

Is there a certain number of hours needed to work for the site? If so, how many?

What is included in the RV site? Water? Sewage? Electricity (specify amps available)? Cable? Wi-Fi?

If electricity is provided, is this unlimited usage, or is there an allowance allotted for the site a month? What is this allowance?

How many days a week will each person be working? Are we working the same days/hours? Are we off the same days?

How many hours does one typically work a week? What is the rate of pay per hour?

Is there an opportunity to work overtime? What is the rate of pay for this?

Is a laundry allowance given? What is this amount?

If propane or store-bought items are sold by the company, is a discount offered for employees?

For income tax purposes, are we considered employees of the company or independent contractors? Is the RV site taxed?

For office work, including online programs, what type of software does your company use? Is there an opportunity to preview a demo of this program or attend a training either before or upon arrival of the job position?

What is the dress code? Is a uniform provided?

What would be the best ways for us to prepare for the weather in that region of the country at that time of year? What should we be aware of or bring to help acclimate to the environment? (This can encompass proper clothing for weather changes, insect/bug exposure, and RV preparation, to name a few adjustments.)

Since we are traveling with our pets, we always make sure they are welcomed and ask about the company rules regarding pets in the campground (e.g., leash length, access to a dog run, cleaning up after pets, regulations of breed, weight, or number of pets).

What is the preferred arrival date? How soon can we arrive at the site? Do we pay for the RV site if we show up before the contracted date?

It is important to obtain as much information as you can from the interview to make a calculated decision. It is also equally, if not more important, to put your best foot forward with each interview, showing professionalism and tact. Being prepared with talking points, keeping appointments, sounding upbeat, avoiding slang terminology and profanity, are essential ways you can demonstrate these attributes.

DON'T FORGET TO FOLLOW-UP

Before we conclude our phone or video chat interview, we make sure to thank them for the opportunity to learn more about the company and position and for the chance to share a little bit more about ourselves. If the interviewer hasn't mentioned yet, we ask a few final questions.

What are the next steps in the hiring process?

Are there any additional pieces of information about our work experience they would like us to send (i.e., certifications, examples of publications)?

When should we expect to hear back from them?

Employers generally have a list of potential candidates to interview, so it could take a few days to a week before we receive a follow-up phone call or email. Either way, we always send an email within 24 hours of our interview, along with any additional information they request. In our follow-up email, we thank them for the interview opportunity again and express our excitement in hearing back from them.

If we are offered a position, we are usually sent a preliminary contract to review and sign. It's a virtual handshake agreeing to show up and commit to the season. Typically, the contracts are meant to summarize what was discussed during the interview: the length of employment, job duties, and compensation package. Although we prefer having some sort of written workamping agreement, this is not always what ends up happening. Two of our former employers sealed the deal with a mutual agreement over the phone.

We make it a point to keep in touch with the company before beginning the new job. We email any additional questions that come up in the interim and give them updates on our travels to their location. Our contact is ensuring that we have continued interest and commitment to the job, and we can be relied on.

As explained in the interview portion, this step is not necessarily a part of all application processes, at least not as extensive as others. The essential components in any application process are to follow the work ad as specified, keep with the deadlines turning in items requested by the employer, and do your part to follow-up! Always be prepared on your end.

SECTION FOUR:

Additional Thoughts About
Seasonal Workamping

ORIENTATION AND TRAINING

With every new workamping job comes the obligatory orientation and training protocols. This usually begins a day or two after we arrive at our location and settle into our RV site. For the most part, we typically stay at a campground during the duration of our workamping jobs. The only exception was in Tennessee, where we were parked in a huge field during our time as holiday lot managers.

Orientation is always a mishmash of paperwork to be completed and signed. On rare occasions, these forms are completed online, either at the job site or before arriving. Every company has its own procedures. For our part, we make sure to ask how we can prepare for this part of the hiring process and bring any requested items to the meeting.

Since this process usually involves filling out state and federal tax forms, we come prepared with required forms of identification, whether it's a passport or a combination of a driver's license and social security card. We have also signed contract agreements during orientation. These forms stipulated our duties, company policies, and compensation for the time that we were employed. We always review these contracts and make changes or clarify portions with the employer then and there.

Oftentimes, employers will use this initial meeting time to take employees on a tour of the campground or facility, depending on your work location. Whether we are taking a stroll through a winery, riding on a golf cart through a campground, or watching a video about the beet harvest, our guide will usually give us a brief background about their establishment and a general layout of the worksite.

Other preliminary matters that are addressed during orientation are official job assignments, work schedules, and issuing work uniforms (e.g., company shirts). We take this time to ask questions pertaining to our living arrangements, daily routines, and work specifics. If we are working at a campground, we could usually refer to the park brochure for information on park rules, Wi-Fi access code, and hours that amenities are open to campers. If we are new to a location, we want to know where to access essential supplies and services like local grocery stores, laundromats, and RV supply shops.

Depending on the complexity of the job, a day to a week is set aside for training. Training takes the form of instructional videos, mini class tutorials, and on-the-job practice. We have watched back to back videos regarding subjects like problem-solving among employees and customers, workplace harassment, safety on the job, and specific job assignments. Classroom time or on-the-job training is typically specific to the job assignment.

Amazon CamperForce has a rather in-depth safety school for all employees. We were introduced to (or for those of us returning, given a review of) the type of equipment used on a regular basis. We were guided through a series of modules that showed us how to interpret signs and taped off areas. After demonstrating how to properly utilize and maneuver through our workspace, we were given the opportunity to practice. It was not the most riveting of courses but a necessary one in such a busy environment.

Training on the job site can be very intense, especially if you are new to the position, and it requires multiple tasks to be completed throughout the day. Jobs like front desk receptionist at a campground involve learning the ins and outs of a software program, familiarizing yourself with products and services utilized by the company, and enforcing park policies daily. Since campground managers see different workampers each season, they usually have procedures and routines in places to create some form of uniformity. Employees are sometimes provided with a checklist of daily chores and tasks to complete during your shift. One campground had an entire binder of procedures to refer to for various situations that might occur in the office and with outside maintenance.

Some workamping jobs like Amazon CamperForce and the sugar beet harvest ease their employees into regular work weeks, having them train for a fraction of the time they would normally work each day. This is so each worker has the opportunity to acclimate to the work environment (e.g., loud noises, weather conditions) and being on their feet for hours at a time. In contrast, at Prairie Berry Winery, we were behind the bar talking about and serving wine to small groups of tourists within a matter of a day or two after training.

We try to take full advantage of training days by asking many questions and posing possible troublesome scenarios to maximize learning. The learning process extends beyond training, sometimes through trial and error, especially in a campground job where it seems like almost every day can pose a different customer concern or troubleshooting situation. Every job and every workamper experiences their own learning curve.

HOW WORKAMPING
AFFECTS INCOME TAXES

Two things are certain in life, death and taxes. When we first started looking into workamping, tax questions came up frequently. How do we deal with taxes in multiple states? If we get a site for free, does that count as income, and if so, are we taxed at the value of that site? Other tax questions mounted.

We thought we would need to find a special person to prepare our taxes each year because workamping had to complicate them to a point where we surely couldn't handle the process ourselves. It turns out, after five years of filing our taxes as full-time RVers, tax software like TurboTax made it possible to get through tax season with a minimal amount of antacids.

Before I get into taxes, I do feel it's important to say that I am not a tax expert, and if you have specific tax questions related to your unique tax situation, it is always recommended to consult a professional.

Choosing the Right Domicile

As a US citizen, it is required by law that you establish a state of residency. This 'home base' or domicile is your permanent address and has many legal purposes. Domicile plays a key role in paying taxes, voting, and collecting benefits.

Many full-timers choose to register in states that have no state income taxes, low property taxes, lower vehicle registration charges, and inexpensive insurance payments. There are a few states that are popular with RVers to "live" in like Texas, Florida, and South Dakota. One of the reasons RVers choose one of these states is because they don't have a state income tax, and are also very RV friendly.

Choosing one domicile over another is generally a personal choice with many criteria involved. If you have any domicile questions, I recommend checking out Escapees RV Club's website. They have multiple articles about domicile choice, and we used them to get our address in Texas. Check out escapees.com/category/domicile/ for more information on that subject. There are other companies that help RVers with domicile choices. If you choose to domicile in South Dakota, Dakota Post is another resource that can walk you through the process, including registering your vehicle. Their website is dakotapost.net.

Working in Other States

As a workamper, you will probably end up working in many states that collect state income tax. You will owe those states their piece of the pie. States have different income tax laws for out-of-state workers which can affect your refund in that state. Ultimately, you are responsible for paying taxes on the income you earned in any state.

You don't have to memorize every state's tax laws. With TurboTax, for example, I input my income information like W-2s into their system, and it will recognize the different states I worked in. The program not only walks me through my federal taxes, but it also tells me which states I should file in and details that state's filing process.

W-2

Most of our workamping jobs have considered us employees and give us a W-2 form in January. There are a couple of ways they have sent this form. Some have sent us emails containing a way to digitally download the form while most mailed our forms to our home address in Texas. We use the Escapees mail forwarding service, so all we have to do is have our mail sent to wherever we are in mid-February.

1099

Some businesses paid us as independent contractors. An example would be the holiday lot. As an independent contractor, you'll receive a 1099 form if you earned more than $600 during your work stint. Ultimately, you are required by law to claim all income, regardless if the business remits any forms or receipts.

Remember, if you work a job as an independent contractor, taxes are not subtracted from your paychecks. You will be responsible for paying the taxes when you file them. Of course, the IRS is generally willing to accept your money, so you can pay ahead of time what you think your tax burden may be from any contractor work you do. I have never done this, but it's possible. You are also responsible for claiming that income in the state you made it in.

Deductions

Current tax law doesn't allow you to claim many deductions on W-2 work, but if you have your own business or work as an independent contractor, many expenses are deductible. It is important to keep records and receipts of all expenses for your business. Keep track of mileage in a logbook or spreadsheet.

We pay for a tier of TurboTax that also includes an app called QuickBooks Self Employed. The app connects to our bank accounts and tracks our mileage. Once a week, I will go through all the trips and transactions and categorize them as business or personal. At the end of the year, the app syncs with TurboTax to do most of the deduction work for me.

Are RV sites considered taxable income?

We ask this question to all of our employers. The answer is not always clear, but most of the time, an RV site is not considered taxable income. I'm going to quote the 2019 Publication 525,

Taxable & NonTaxable Income from the irs.gov website. Under Meals and Lodging it states:

"You don't include in your income the value of meals and lodging provided to you and your family by your employer at no charge if the following conditions are met..."

The lodging is:

a. Furnished on the business premises of your employer,

b. Furnished for the convenience of your employer, and

c. A condition of your employment. (You must accept it in order to be able to properly perform your duties.)"

So far, we have not claimed an RV site as a taxable income in almost 6 years. That isn't to say that it is possible to get into a situation where you are legally obligated to claim a free site as taxable income, but it is definitely rare.

Final Thoughts on Filing Taxes

Some higher tiers of TurboTax allow you to speak to a certified tax person either via phone or chat window. They can walk you through any tax questions and review the paperwork. If you would rather go to someone to have them do your taxes, it is possible to find a knowledgeable CPA to help you file.

FUNDING YOUR TRAVELS THROUGH SEASONAL WORKAMPING

Everyone's financial situation is different. We know some workampers who do fine on $1400 a month and sometimes less. We also know others who tend to spend a lot more. I can attest to the fact that workamping will probably not make you rich, and you will probably not always work your dream job. There are a few things to consider when planning to become a seasonal workamper.

First, if you are planning on making a living workamping seasonal jobs, it is important to have a realistic idea of how much you will make. As you have already seen above, the average workamping position pays around $10 to $12 an hour. Some jobs pay more than that or have a lot of overtime pay.

Second, you are not going to magically change your in-grained habits or lifestyle when you move into an RV. If you like to go out and eat three nights a week, you will probably enjoy going out to eat often even after moving into an RV. If you like going to movies, you will still want to do that. Some people will want to have their ESPN or other cable/satellite channels they enjoy watching. You will still have a TV service bill in that case. Make sure your budget is realistic for your unique lifestyle.

Create a monthly budget using a spreadsheet. Consider expenses you will have living in your RV. These may include items like groceries, fuel, entertainment, RV or tow vehicle payments, phone/internet charges, health insurance, etc. Having a monthly budget, which includes realistic expenses based on your current spending, will help you determine how much you need to make from workamping jobs.

Now change the budget based on your workamping job. For example, to rent an RV site for a month at a moderate RV park, it costs about $500. I want to account for that in my budget, but if the job I'm taking covers the site with all hours paid, I can remove that from my budget. Below is an example budget we once had.

Month-to-Month

RV Payment	$400
Internet/Smart Phone Coverage through Verizon	$200
Health Insurance	$200
RV site	$500
Fuel	$50-$200
Groceries	$400
Pet Costs	$100
Entertainment	$300
Miscellaneous (e.g., repairs, utilities at site, propane, vet visits)	$200

From the budget above, you can see that we would need to pull in a minimum of $2500 a month. However, if our job provides a site that drops to $2000 a month. We can vary the total of other items. For example, we don't travel as much or as far once we get to a workamping job. This would decrease our fuel usage. On the flip side, if we need to make a repair on the RV, this may increase our monthly total. By having an idea of what we spend on average per month, we can more accurately decide if any given job (including perks) will cover our expenses.

Obviously, everyone's version of what is comfortable differs. Like all budgets, this one will grow or shrink depending upon our circumstances. We certainly aren't living a lavish lifestyle or striking it rich workamping, but we are continuing to enjoy the journey and live a life that, at one time, we didn't think was possible.

Finally, the third tidbit I would like to leave you with is the importance of multiple streams of income. Sometimes our seasonal workamping jobs barely cover our monthly expenses, and we aren't able to put any extra away for a rainy day. By having additional forms of income, we can put a little more away at a time and save up for retirement, unexpected expenses like medical emergencies and vehicle repairs, and time off in between workamping gigs.

Besides seasonal workamping, we pull in additional paychecks via our blog and freelance writing for various publications. We have also worked odd jobs like pet sitting, weed whacking, and performing a magic show. We've offered to work extra hours at a workamping job. Natalie worked one spring as a substitute teacher with a school district in addition to our camp host job in Nevada. I have a side job where I test websites and apps for companies online. These additional sources can create a nice cushion.

LESSONS WE'VE LEARNED AS SEASONAL WORKAMPERS

We recently celebrated our fifth year as full-time RVers. Many RVers mark these yearly occasions as "nomadversaries." We reflected on our time on the road and realized that in such a short time, we have experienced so much change: changes in scenery, people, RV repairs and mishaps, and jobs. However, one thing that has remained constant is our means of living, seasonal workamping. In that time, we have learned so much about this aspect of RVing, both its benefits and setbacks.

There is no shortage of workamping jobs. One of our biggest worries about full-time RVing was how to finance our new lifestyle, especially since we did not have remote jobs, and we were decades from retirement. We were unsure where the seasonal workamping job market stood or what employers were seeking in potential workers.

Turns out, jobs in and around the nation are in abundance and employers are thirsty for help. We usually have jobs set up six months to a year in advance, and they almost always offer an RV site free of charge and pay that meets our budget needs.

Although most jobs ask for couples or two person teams, there are plenty of jobs available for single workampers. It may take a little more looking to find them, but they are there.

As we have already mentioned, there are many resources that you can turn to for seasonal job ads. There are also quite a few RV-related forums and Facebook groups advertising jobs throughout the year.

We have come across a minor setback with finding an

abundance of workamping jobs. Although workamping jobs are available throughout the year, with every season, we have noticed slim pickings between January and April. Many businesses are slowing down after the holidays and don't need extra help. Work is available but not necessarily in the locations or with a job you are interested in. Many RVers take time off from workamping during this time. They head south to the warmer climate and time on the beach or in the desert.

Workamping allows us to meet all kinds of people. RVers are some of the most helpful, friendly people you will meet on the road. Many are happy to lend a hand with RV troubleshooting, give travel advice, suggest a new workamping job, and refer you to sources for additional guidance like books, websites, stores, or apps. Then there are the potlucks and stories around the campfire. RVers love sharing their adventures on the road. Oftentimes, their stories have lessons that apply to your own experiences.

Some fellow workampers have become lifelong friends and we keep in contact regularly. Even though the RVing community is large in numbers, it is small in the way that you have many opportunities to meet up, work together again, or meet someone that knows your RV buddies.

Treat each workamping job as a learning experience. Each job has its challenges. Every time we take on one of these challenges, we learn something new. It's not always a new skill. We learn about different professions like winemaking, farming, retail, and hospitality. Each new bit of knowledge gives us a slightly wider picture of all the moving parts of our country's industries and how they fit together. The lessons we learn can be brought with us to make our jobs easier, and sometimes we get to share some of those ideas with another business and make their life easier too.

Sometimes a job isn't all it's cracked up to be. Eventually, all workampers get to a job that is completely different from what was described. I was once told that a job that paid $8 an hour was mostly camp host stuff and required some light landscaping. I arrived to find myself working heavy machinery, digging trenches, planting over 200 trees, and reshaping an area of a forest with thousands of pounds of rock and gravel. I didn't mind the work, I just felt I was getting the short end of the stick on pay.

As most of us have encountered at one time or another, be it work, school, or clubs, anytime you have many people with different personalities and life experiences, sometimes it can be challenging for everyone to get along. We have arrived at places to find the environment somewhat hostile and unfriendly to the workers. Sometimes, employees bring enough personal baggage to turn the workplace into a drama-filled soap opera. Other times, we have found that the group of people put together for a season doesn't work well together.

What do we do in those situations? For the most part, we try to stick it out if we can. If it is possible to go to a manager with a problem, we do. If it's something we must work out on our own, we take the necessary steps. Our goal is to fulfill our commitments, and we don't want to burn bridges. Most positions only last for a matter of months, and we don't have to return to any jobs that we don't want to. If a situation becomes particularly bad, our house does have wheels.

Take advantage of the large and small things to do at your next workamping gig. Our country is diverse in landscape and culture and often reflected in the area's main attractions-national and state parks, museums, and amusement parks. Workamping jobs take us to many popular destinations. We make sure to check off these bucket list items during our stay, but we also give equal attention to the local scene.

We try to participate in local events or organizations. We joined a sci-fi group in Kansas that met monthly to plan community projects and talk about Star Trek episodes. We scheduled meetups with a local scuba diving group weekly and dove in the Great Lakes. We volunteered at the Humane Society, walking dogs and snuggling with cats. We've tried all kinds of regional dishes at farmer's markets and local dives and have attended all kinds of festivals and celebrations in nearby towns.

Seasonal workamping has opened up new experiences and possibilities for our travels. We've only scratched the surface and have a whole list of job opportunities we have yet to try. We will continue to grow and learn as we add more workamping jobs and places to our resume.

CONCLUSION

That's how we did it and continue to do it. Every time we tell someone who isn't an RVer what we do, they are astonished that it's possible. Our story, and the fact that there are thousands of workampers around the nation, is a testament to the fact that it is possible to fund your travels through seasonal workamping. I'll tell you what I tell everyone else. It's certainly not a way to get rich, but we get to see the country.

We have talked to many other workampers, and though there are similarities in how we find and apply for jobs, everyone does this for different reasons. They follow their own path, find their own groove, and answer their own questions as to why they want to pick up their life and take it, well, everywhere. We started this crazy adventure hoping to figure out where we might eventually want to live.

We hope that at this point, you have a better understanding of seasonal workamping, how to find and apply for jobs, and what to expect out of the hiring process. We hope that sharing a bit of our story might just inspire you to go out on the open road and start your own workamping adventures.

If you have further questions, check us out at HenleysHappyTrails.com. You can get in touch with us using the "Contact Us" page of our site. Thank you again for reading and happy trails!

GLOSSARY OF LINKS

RV Blogs

Henley's Happy Trails | A Couples Search for Health, Happiness and Home in Their RV

https://henleyshappytrails.com

RV Dreams | Could RV Living Be Your Dream? Let's Find Out!!

https://rv-dreams.com

Domicile Questions

Escapees| Domicile Archives

https://www.escapees.com/category/domicile/

Dakota Post | Mail Forwarding Service

https://dakotapost.net/

Find Workamping Jobs

Workamper News | The Original Resource Of Jobs For RVers, Since 1987!

https://workamper.com/

CoolWorks | Cool summer jobs and seasonal jobs in the great outdoors

https://www.coolworks.com/

PeakSeason | Find Seasonal Jobs in Extraordinary Locations

https://www.peakseason.com/

Workers On Wheels | Work for RVers and Campers

https://www.work-for-rvers-and-campers.com/

Happy Vagabonds | RV Camping, Campgrounds and Work Camper Jobs

http://www.happyvagabonds.com

WorkingCouples.com | The Single Largest Source of Jobs for Couples Anywhere!

https://workingcouples.com/

WorkampingJobs.com - Free Job Listings from Campgrounds and RV Parks

https://workampingjobs.com/

Work At KOA | Find Workamper Jobs at KOAs

https://workatkoa.com/

American Land & Leisure| Manage campgrounds, picnic areas, and boat ramps for the USDA Forest Service, PG&E and California State Parks

http://www.americanll.com

Volunteer.gov | America's Natural and Cultural Resources Volunteer Portal

https://www.volunteer.gov/

Habitat for Humanity | RV Care-A-Vanners

https://www.habitat.org/volunteer/travel-and-build/rv-care-a-vanners

Sugar Beet Harvest | The Unbeetable Experience

https://www.theunbeetableexperience.com/

Amazon CamperForce | Jobs for RVers and Work Campers

https://www.amazondelivers.jobs/about/camperforce/

www.ingramcontent.com/pod-product-compliance
Lightning Source LLC
Chambersburg PA
CBHW072017150726
47999CB00002B/705